DISCERNING DITCHES IN THE LAST DAYS

(New Edition)

I0143246

REV (DR) TUNDE BOLANTA

Restoration Bible Church and Ministries,

©Tunde Bolanta

First Published 1995
This Edition 2018

ISBN: 978-1-907095-30-6

For more copies, write to:
The Publication Department,
Restoration Bible Church & Ministries, Inc.,
P. O. Box 1485, Kaduna, Nigeria.

This Edition of *"Discerning Ditches in the Last Days"* is published by
Winning Faith Publications,
London. UK

CONTENTS

DEDICATION

This book is dedicated to:
Tina, my dear wife, whose quiet strength and stability have been a stabilizing factor in my life; Nathan and Sharon and Ephraim my lovely children and my parents, John and Elizabeth Bolanta, who have given me a Godly heritage.

PREFACE

Every believer who is sensitive to the Holy-Spirit knows that we are on the cutting edge of an unprecedented move of God. It seems that when the Lord plans revival Satan tries to have one also, by copying and counterfeiting the real and genuine, so that people will either shy away from the real or 'muddy' up the waters of God's revival through fleshly moves.

It dawned on me after a divine encounter when the Lord Jesus showed himself to me in a vision in 1991, I was privileged to see the imminent catching away or rapture of the church.

This book is intended to help us as we await his coming for we must not be side-tracked. I believe change comes from the top. God will change the hearts of his ministers so that we in turn by the washing of "water by the word" would minister to His body, the church. There are minor points of which all will never agree but there are important areas we need understanding in order that we may fulfill our roles accurately and effectively as we wait His appearing:

ACTS 6:7: *"And the word of the God increased; and the number of the disciples multiplied in Jerusalem greatly; and a great company of the Priests were obedient to the faith".*

CHAPTER 1

STRANGE FIRES

"And Nadab and Abihu, the sons of Aaron, took either of them his censer, and put fire therein, and put incense thereon, and offered strange fire before the LORD, which he commanded them not. And there went out fire from the LORD, and devoured them, and they died before the LORD. Then Moses said unto Aaron,

This is it that the LORD spake saying I will be sanctified in them that come nigh me, and before all the people I will be glorified And Aaron held his peace. And Moses called Mishael and Elzaphan, the sons of Uzziel the uncle of Aaron, and said unto them, Come near carry your brethren from before the sanctuary out of the camp. So they went near and carried them in their coats out of the camp; as Moses had said. And Moses said unto Aaron, and unto Eleazar and unto Ithamar, his sons, Uncover not your heads, neither rend your clothes; lest ye die and lest wrath come upon all the people: but let your brethren, the whole house of Israel, bewail the burning which the LORD hath kindled.

And ye shall not go out from the door of the tabernacle of the congregation, lest ye die for the anointing oil of the LORD is upon you. And they did according to the word of Moses". **Leveticus 10:1-7**

The above passage is a graphic reminder that God does not compromise his standards; he does not conform to man's wishes and is not respecter of persons.

Although Nadab and Abihu were priests and sons of Aaron the High priest God did not spare them. The mercies of God in the new covenant has been the saving grace because strange fires are not uncommon in some places they have usurped real worship.

The word of God and true worship is substituted for anything that draws the crowd and produce quick gain. Strange fires cause the real presence of God to disappear, opening doors to familiar spirits to hold sway.

History has shown that once the word of God is substituted for experiences and unscriptural revelations the power of God wanes and man is open for deception. The Holy Spirit who is the power of God was sent to confirm the word of God and lift up Jesus. The replacement of the word of God with human revelations and ideas caused the church to descend into the dark ages.

Thank God for the work of reformers who made the word available to us again and through them the light of God, his presence and power began to manifest. Men like John Wycliffe, John Hus, Martin Luther, John Knox among others who risked their lives to bring the light.

In the body of Christ, we have increasing cases of ministers who come up with prophetic revelations that have no biblical precedence or New Testament basis but have results to back up their claim. The word of God has been given to us as a denominator, as an x-ray machine to help us decipher what is God what is man and what is demonic.

More worrying is the fact that many of the revelations and attendant practices are very similar with cultic practices in traditional religions but the desperation and desire to see quick answers have made many not to ask questions. The general statement used to explain things away is to say "the Lord has revealed to me specially" or "the Lord said".

TYPES AND SHADOWS
The Old Testament was a covenant for God fearing but spiritually dead people because Jesus is the first person to be born again from death to life. When Jesus e became sin for us., he died spiritually but was raised from the dead.
In reaching the people of God in the Old Testament God had to do it from outside, their holiness was demonstrated externally. God set up a tabernacle for them patterned after the heavenly one for sacrifice, he gave them the Passover which was a type of Christ.

The old testament looked to the cross, we who are recreated in Christ cannot follow Old testament practices to receive righteousness neither can we obtain the blessings of God through adherence to Old testament types and shadows thereby despising the cross and the blood of redemption.

Peter at the beautiful gate said faith in Christ is what made the lame man healed. When we focus on types and shadows, our faith can be misplaced, our practices become works done in the flesh and not of faith and rest in the finished work of Christ, furthermore we risk being hood winked by cultic people who use similar emblems and objects thereby destroying our faith.

"The Holy Ghost this signifying that the way into the holiest of all was not yet made manifest while as the first tabernacle was yet standing: Which was a figure for the time then present in which were offered both gifts and sacrifices, that could not make him that did the service perfect as pertaining to the conscience; Which stood only in meats and drinks, and divers washings, and carnal

ordinances, imposed on them until the time of reformation". **Hebrews 9:8-10**

Many things have been abolished for the New Testament believer, all the ceremonial washings, the tabernacle, numerous laws and other ordinances. Jesus demonstrated that faith in God is the way to receive the blessing of God.

He went about teaching, preaching and healing the sick. Jesus did not go about distributing candles, oil, water, soap, Peppermint, mantles, threads, sand, honey and other emblems as a way to receive miracles. He based his ministry on the word not on articles and emblems and he was the transition between the Old and the New Testament.

The drift towards fetishes and darkness is not new, this happened before in church history.

This is similar to the way the Gnostics of old operated, smuggling many false revelations into the church. In order to receive satellite signals to your television you need specified decoders to pick up the signals, depending on what stations you want to receive, some decoders and sensors won't pick up certain signals no matter how hard you tried.

It is the word that guarantees that the input we are getting is from the Holy-Spirit, the fact that one experiences a miracle is no guarantee that the manifestation is from God. It all depends on the channel you are tuned in from.

There is no telling what information will pour into your home if you were tuned to a station you don't like because of a wrong decoder or mistakenly tuning into a wrong channel or frequency.

"These were more noble than those in Thessalonica, in that they received the word with all readiness of mind, and searched the scriptures daily, whether those things were so". **Ac 17:11**

The Berean Christians were nobler because they went and searched if what they heard was so. The Bible is the constitution of the kingdom of God, a person who immigrates into a new nation has to abide by their laws your station in life notwithstanding, if they drive on the left you cannot say the Lord revealed to you specially to drive on the left if you do so you will get killed and also endanger the life of others.

Spiritual suicide is the result when we decide to make our own laws and do our own revelation; God will not change his word for anybody.

The following excerpts shed more light on why the church descended into the dark ages, as the Gnostics manufactured their own revelations at will and the church failed to use the word as the basis of her experience.

After the death of the early apostles the church shifted from sound doctrines she sought signs and wonders, experiences, quick results over relationship with the Lord and descended into the dark ages.

When there is a vacuum the enemy tries to fill it would appear that with the home going of the first apostles, there seemed to be no apostolic oversight and the false revelators took the day.

MERCHANDISING THE ANOINTING

During the First Century, when the original apostles were alive and ministering, there was a heavy emphasis on apostolic teaching — which eventually became the New testament scriptures. At this time, there was an abundance of signs, wonders, miracles and divers gifts of the Holy Spirit.

Then toward the end of the First Century, and into the middle of the Second Century, when the apostles were gone, Paul's prediction began to be fulfilled. "Grievous wolves" entered in among the flock.

This is when these strange forms of Gnosticism began to take hold of the Church. With the strong leadership of the apostles out of the way, these fraudulent ministers with ulterior motives began to make in-roads into the Church at an alarming rate of speed.

Respect for the Word of God had deteriorated to such an extent, that the faithful bishop Polycarp, known as "the great teacher of Asia," in regard to Paul's writings, said: "I am persuaded that ye are well-trained in the sacred writings, and nothing is hidden from you. But to myself this is not granted."

In other words, this well-known bishop who was called "the great teacher of Asia," was for all practical purposes unfamiliar with Paul's writings by his own admission! The spiritual atmosphere of the Church began to rapidly decline as people moved away from the teaching of the apostles toward other so-called "deep things". Over a period of time, the foundational teachings of the apostles were nearly discarded, and an abnormal emphasis to receive brand new revelation came into a place of prominence. Remove the Word, Remove the Power.

At first, this departure from the Word took place very slowly. Thus, there was still enough Word being preached at beginning of the First Century for the Holy Spirit to confirm with signs and wonders.

But eventually, this drifting away from the Word became so gross, so far removed from the message the apostles preached, so far off into strange and curious teachings, that there was no longer enough Word being preached for the Holy Spirit to confirm.

Church history reveals that the strong teachings of the apostles had almost been entirely replaced. Gnostic messages ecclesiastical structures, orthodoxy unrelated to scripture and apostolic pattern, legalism and other such things, had usurped the place of the Word.

It wasn't long after these changes began to be accepted and practiced (circa. A.D. 260) that the gifts and power of the Holy Spirit ceased to function in the Church. The strong presence of the Spirit was attached to the strong teaching of the Word. When the Word was gone, the Spirit's power was gone too.

This departing from "the faith" in pursuit of greater spiritual experiences eventually robbed them of the very thing that they were seeking: God's power.

With the teaching of the Word gone, the power and gifts of the Holy Spirit disappeared and spiritual darkness began to fill the Church. Soon after this, the world was ushered into that horribly dark chapter in history which we call "The Dark Ages."

From time to time after this, there would be occasional revivals of supernatural power. Every time this occurred, it happened during a period when the Word of God was being re-emphasized. This brought the gifts and power of the Spirit back into the church.

Therefore, if we want power, we must learn a lesson from history and stick to the Word. These two — the Word and power — are inseparable. ."

HOLY SPIRIT IN A BOTTLE?

"Nevertheless, I tell you the truth; It is expedient for you that I go away for if I go not away the Comforter will not come unto you; but if I depart I will send him unto you. And when he is come he will reprove the world of sin, and of righteousness, and of judgment: Of sin, because they believe not on me; Of righteousness, because I go to my Father, and ye see me no more; Of judgment, because the prince of this world is judged. I have yet many things to say unto you, but ye cannot bear them now. Howbeit when he, the Spirit of truth,

is come he will guide you into all truth: for he shall not speak of himself; but whatsoever he shall hear that shall he speak and he will shew you things to come.
He shall glorify me: for he shall receive of mine, and shall shew it unto you. All things that the Father hath are mine: therefore said I that he shall take of mine, and shall shew it unto you. **John 16: 7-15**

The teaching that the Holy Spirit is in the anointing oil bottle carried by some Christians has no basis in the word of God.

The Holy Spirit is likened to oil but he is not oil, in fact He is a person. Jesus said, when "He the Spirit of truth comes". The Holy Spirit is likened to a dove but he is not a dove, the Holy Spirit is likened to wind but he is not the wind. If he is the oil in the anointing bottle then every oil bottle carries God, which is not so.

One of the challenges the reformers like Martin Luther had was to correct the teaching that when you took the Holy Communion you are actually eating the body and drinking the blood of Jesus. This is similar to what is taught that the representation of a thing in the scripture turns into the real thing. If it was really possible to bottle the Holy Spirit, then everyone will like to take their bottles everywhere, for those who hold this teaching the bottle of oil is always handy to solve problems. Jesus said, the Spirit will dwell in the believer he did not teach that we would carry him around in a bottle.

DRINKING ANOINTING OIL

Oil is symbolically a type of the spirit in the Bible. There are some scriptural New and Old Testament use of oil. Oil is used for anointing people into offices of ministry (Ex 30:31; Ex 37:39) to anoint the sick (James 5:14-16).

Some ask believers to drink olive oil for their prosperity and anoint everything with oil. People have been known to anoint guns, cutlasses and machetes with oil to fight their enemies.

To teach that God has put the Holy- Spirit in a bottle is heretical. How can the creation of God bottle the creator of the universe? The logic of this argument stands on its head at best puerile and faulty. This thinking creates the impression that you can use the Holy-spirit like you would your favorite medication or utensil. He becomes a one size fits all solution.

OIL IS SYMBOLIC OF THE SPIRIT; IT IS NOT THE SPIRIT.

In the Old Testament, some anointing were symbolized by long hair which was not supposed to be cut. An example is Samson's anointing of strength (Nazarenes never cut their hair).

To ask anyone who wanted an anointing to wear long dreadlocks is putting people in bondage. There are religions that still practice this today but this not a New Testament teaching.

One of the major differences between the Old Testament and New Testament is that the former deals with types - a fore shadowing - because the people were spiritually dead, all they did and all they had been a shadow of the real. We have the real in the new. It is the word of God in our human spirit energized by the Holy Spirit that produces result. The word in our heart is what produces result, and not just oil on the flesh.

In the New Testament we worship in the spirit, not in the flesh (Phil 3:3). It is the word of God in the human spirit which produces HEALING, MIRACLES, PROTECTION, PROSPERITY, and so on. Olive oil cannot mix with your human spirit. It is clay on clay (John 6:63) - the words I speak are spirit and life.

To use the anointing oil as a magic wand and as a cure all solution it is removing the emphasis from the word to something you can feel and touch. The abuse puts the emphasis on the element not on the word of God, the Bible says the elders praying for the sick should anoint with oil but the prayer of faith is what saves the sick, not the oil.

The oil in this instance would be a point of contact, symbolic of the Holy Spirit as the believer releases faith in God's word.

People will not leave their homes without anointing themselves and their children, some will only enter their cars when it has been anointed, in a hotel they will anoint the walls to ward off evil, some even put anointing oil in the food they eat.

It has become a talisman. In the new covenant the believer has some one more powerful than oil; he is the Holy-Spirit who raised Jesus from the dead and no demonic power could stop the resurrection, therefore the word in your heart and mouth and the ever-present power of the Holy Spirit will bring changes.

It might seem easier and it requires no intimacy with God to quickly anoint your fore head in a crises situation leaving the word of God and the Holy Spirit out.

As a result of the fetish and cultic background of some believers before they came to faith in Jesus where the emphasis was on deliverance through certain elements, this sort of teaching appeals to the flesh. Bogus testimonies are often given of incredible things happening but we must be reminded that the realm of the Spirit is filled with familiar spirits who can also manifest.

There is no New Testament scripture for many of the doctrines on oil been preached? Oil in scripture is symbolic of the Holy-Spirit but not the Holy-Spirit as it is being taught today. We can anoint the sick with oil, we can set people apart for ministry by anointing them, in the case of the sick it is the prayer of faith that saves the sick not the gallons of oil the sick consumes. God takes us back to the word because faith comes through the word of God.

The Old Testament saints were spiritually dead people because they were not born again, so God had to deal with them from the outside. That explains why there were so many laws to help them keep the external.

In the New Testament we are to allow the word to abide in our spirits richly (Col3:16-17); the word energized by the Holy Spirit brings the desired result. If you drank oil for the next thirty years it would never get into your spirit because oil is a physical material. It is the word in the human spirit that produces result.

Some have argued that oil is merely a point of contact. It is true that the Bible talks of anointing the sick with oil (James 5:16) it does not say anything about drinking it. If you are to use this as the only basis, the use is to anoint, not drink. You cannot see in the New Testament any record of believers drinking anointed oil for their need.

In James 5:16 it is the prayer of faith that saves the sick, and not the oil. To put your emphasis on oil as an all -purpose cure is to follow a magic formula. It bothers on witchcraft.

If the Lord in a situation had given someone a specific word to use anointing oil in a special way, this cannot be taught as a doctrine. Should you receive a prophetic direction to use oil or any other thing as a point of contact it is unscriptural to teach it as a doctrine to all. A prophetic word to you cannot be a word to all. The word of knowledge is given to one not to all.

Jesus told his disciples to go to and get tax money from a fish mouth, this does not mean any time we need money we all go fishing. Jesus put mud on a man's eye and he was healed, does this mean we should use mud for healing the sick; a personal word cannot become doctrine and supersede the written word.

Jesus said there were many widows in the days of Elijah but he was only sent to the widow of Zerephath, similarly there were many lepers but Elisha healed Namaan, Jesus said. He is simply saying, the word to one is not the word to all. If you jumped into the Jordan because Namaan did without God saying that to you specifically you will only get wet.

In fact, Namman did not like the specific word to him, because he found it humiliating, God used that method to free him of spiritually leprosy which manifested as pride, what God say to someone may have many reasons that we may not know of. We must not clone miracles let God be God. If God asked you to drink oil in a specific situation the whole church does not need to have an oil drinking service.

"But I tell you of a truth, many widows were in Israel in the days of Elias, when the heaven was shut up three years and six months, when great famine was throughout all the land; But unto none of them was Elias sent save unto Sarepta, a city of Sidon, unto a woman that was a widow. And many lepers were in Israel in the time of Eliseus the prophet; and none of them was cleansed saving Naaman the Syrian". **Luke 4:25-27**

The redemption that Christ has purchased has provided all the blessings of forgiveness, healing and health, deliverance from danger, abundance, the salvation of lost ones.

Our redemption has already happened and as believers spend time in the word there will be manifestation the challenge comes is when there are delays. Instead of running around for quick fix the church must learn to fight the fight of faith.

When the gifts are in operation there may be specific words to individuals and things happen quickly God has sent me to people with prophetic words, told them to do specific things that brought them into great abundance but I could not take that same word and give it to another person.

Time and time again, I have told people within a few months they will finish a building project and supernaturally it happened. I remembered a woman whose children, a set of twins were abducted by a neighbor at age three as I prayed for her the Lord gave a particular date for fulfillment and the woman who abducted them returned them after fourteen years!

The mother of these children did not even know where they were, only God can do a thing like that but it would be dangerous to and criminal to take that same word and give another person with similar needs.

REDEMPTION OF FIRST BORN

This doctrine finds its root in the old- testament which is a type and shadow of the new-testament.

God gave Israel many laws to signify and show their commitment to him, to also show them their need for redemption, as no man could keep the law, there were many sacrifices to keep the relationship.

"And every firstling of an ass thou shalt redeem with a lamb; and if thou wilt not redeem it, then thou shalt break his neck and all the firstborn of man among thy children shalt thou redeem".
Ex 13:13

"But the firstling of an ass thou shalt redeem with a lamb: and if thou redeem him not, then shalt thou break his neck All the firstborn of thy

sons thou shalt redeem And none shall appear before me empty". **Exodus 13:20**

"Everything that openeth the matrix in all flesh, which they bring unto the LORD, whether it be of men or beasts, shall be thine: nevertheless the firstborn of man shalt thou surely redeem and the firstling of unclean beasts shalt thou redeem". **Numbers 18:15**

In the old -testament they were commanded to redeem their first born with an offering, today some ask believers to pay money to redeem their first-born children and themselves if they are a firstborn. It is shocking because Jesus is the first born from the dead and we have our redemption in him.

In the family of God your spiritual heritage supersedes your natural heritage that is why you have no genealogies in the new-testament, after Jesus we are all new creations in the family of God. What Jesus purchased for us as first born of the new creation can never be done with money or any material.

Rom 8:29 ¶ *For whom he did foreknow he also did predestinate to be conformed to the image of his Son, that he might be the firstborn among many brethren.*
"Who is the image of the invisible God, the firstborn of every creature": **Col 1:15**

"And he is the head of the body, the church: who is the beginning, the firstborn from the dead; that in all things he might have the preeminence". **Col 1:18**

Redemption of firstborn teaching and practice is based on the thinking that some first-borns are not doing well in their lives, they are not prosperous because they have not been redeemed through offerings and prayers. All believers needed redemption not only first-born, Christ redeemed all of us from the curse of the law and in our spiritual family Jesus is the first born, he is seated at the right hand of God and we are in him, the church is not under the curse.

If certain negative things become recurring decimals in our lives, we should seek the Lord in prayer, ask others to pray with us but redemption can never be bought by cash it is a shame that this is even suggested because it cost God the life of Jesus to redeem us.

Any time you pay for something that Jesus paid for on the cross you are no longer walking by grace but by works. It amounts to making merchandise of what Jesus gave freely.

"Forasmuch as ye know that ye were not redeemed with corruptible things, as silver and gold, from your vain conversation received by tradition from your fathers; But with the precious blood of Christ, as of a lamb without blemish and without spot": **1 Peter 1:18-19**

This sort of practices that have no precedence in the new testament and challenge the very basis of our redemption are very dangerous to the health of the church, more so when they are connected with money.

We need to be reminded that prior to the reformation there were certain practices that were tied to money, for example some believed giving and buying indulgences will guarantee salvation of loved ones, the church must be careful not to fall into this trap again.

There is nothing new under the sun the devil recycles old errors and his goal is to move us away from the word of God, Jesus and his word are one, when we move away from the word we move away from Jesus.

(The following passage from the book Roaring Reformers shed more light pages 139-140)

"To assist in the payment of these bills, the pope granted the new archbishop of Brandenburg the right to sell indulgences. To expedite the procedure and assure optimum sales, the archbishop hired himself a jest who was gifted in the sale of indulgences. His name was John Tetzel.

He would ride with great pomp to the edge of town; meet there with the town's officials, and then ride ceremoniously to the town square, drawing a crowd as he went. He would plant a large cross bearing the papal arms on it and begin preaching that, with one payment, people could release their relatives from purgatory. He would earnestly manipulate the people:

"God and St. Peter call you. Consider the salvation of your souls and dead loved ones. Are you concerned, considering the temptations etc., whether you will make heaven? Consider your confession here and contributions as a total remission— hear your dead relatives: 'Pity us, pity us...We bore you, nourished you, brought you up, left you our fortunes, and you are so cruel and hard that now you are not willing to set us free.'"

Throughout Germany, the singsongy phrase of Tetzel went forth: "As soon as the coin in the coffer rings the soul from purgatory springs." So many coins were thrown into the coffer that new coins had to be minted on the spot.

When Luther found out about this, he was extremely trouble. The pretense of the indulgence upset"

At this time in church history, a lot of money was raised because the people believed that they could buy the redemption of their loved ones if they paid enough.

The church at this time believed that if you paid enough money you could set the souls of your loved ones free from purgatory. The logic is similar to redeeming first born children; it denies the power and efficacy of the blood of Jesus.

HOLY WATERS AND SODAS

There seems to be a subtle syncretism, an attempt to mix Christianity with cultic practices this has happened because the church has focused on experiences, quick answers not the word of God.

She has focused on elements and fetishes. The sad thing today, is that there is no obvious difference between some churches and herbalist. It is now possible for cults to operate main stream because the emphasis is on wonders not changed lives, Christ-likeness is not the purpose.

I remember a lady who came for prayer several years ago at our church, after praying wither that the Lord would favor her as she headed to the courts for her case the next day, she asked us to give her something to hold on to in court. We replied that she should meditate and speak the scriptures we had given her.

She insisted we should give her some physical material such as oil, handkerchief, and thread. Her faith was obviously not in the word of God but elements, she wanted a talisman.

When cultic practices are carried out in the church, the same spirits operating in those cults come into the church. Once the word is removed there is no light. A cult may run as a church because all some churches focus on are the same element used by cults and not the word of God. If something has no new-testament biblical basis, we must leave it alone. It must not become a doctrine, a way of life for us. We may get results but we open ourselves to evil spirits.

It appears that the enemy is determined to make a mockery of the church that is why the true believer must rise up and stay on the straight and narrow way. In some cultic religions elements like water, sodas such as Coca-Cola, oil, salt, sand, white cloths, honey, are all elements used for prayers. These things are beginning to play central roles in the worship of Christians.

When a pastor ask members to each bring a bottle of Coca-Cola or bring sand from their homes, leaves and branches, hair combs to be prayed on to receive special miracle, that is treading on dangerous grounds.

It is true that God may occasionally give a prophetic direction to a pastor such as in the ministry of Jesus when he told a man to go and wash in the pool of Siloam after he put mud in his eyes but if you study the ministry of Jesus he was not going about applying mud to faces he was teaching, preaching and healing. He put the word first. This was not a daily occurrence; he did not have weekly mud washing service, sand blessing service, Coca-Cola drinking service for healing, mantle waving service, anointing oil drinking service, washing of feet services, getting money from the fish's mouth services, losing the colts services and all the other special manifestations he had were not made into services and doctrines.

Had he done this there would have been uncountable types of services because the Bible says all he did were not recorded because they were too numerous to be recorded.

There is an attempt to blur the lines between true faith and cultism until people can- not know the difference. Familiar spirits are holding sway in many churches because the word of God is not the priority, pastors should not operate like herbalist who distribute fetishes, our goal is to minister the word, teach believers how to stand on the word and have a personal relationship with Jesus, teach them to experience their own victories not eternally tied to the pastors' aprons.

SORTING OUT
A sister in Christ was about to get married and one of the conditions given her was that she needed to be sorted out. This means she needed to go for an extended session where she would give all her life history, filling out a long questionnaire about all her problems, mistakes and sins.

This is a growing practice it is believed that believers need to go through this kind of sessions to be freed of every problem in their lives. This believer has to keep returning for checkup from time to time as you would to a doctor. Life's challenges are usually attributed to something in the past for which the believer needs prayer of deliverance.

The goal of ministry to the oppressed is to feed them the word after prayer so they can learn to stand on their own when the enemy raises his head. To keep the believer returning to a particular spot for checkup is to keep him tied to that place and control their lives.

To focus on sins covered in the blood can cause the believer to come into condemnation, we must not be afraid to deal with things in the past but there is nothing a human being can do about spilt milk in his past the blood of Christ can wipe away the past.

If God has blotted out your sin and does not remember them why do you want to dig up week after week things that God chose to forget. Isaiah 43:25, 1 John 1:9. Why do you need to answer hundreds of questions in order to determine what type of prayer you need? It bothers on psychology and guess work.

The Holy Spirit through the gifts of the spirit can reveal root causes of problem that a lengthy questionnaire about details of life may not show.

There may be need to deal with things in your past but building your life around the past will rob you of your future. I have seen people who have had a very dark past get into the word, receive prayer, and follow a disciplined lifestyle and are totally changed.

Some of the things called demonic are works of the flesh according to Galatians 5:19. Prayers from a minister can never take the place of your decision to put your flesh under.

"But if ye be led of the Spirit, ye are not under the law. Now the works of the flesh are manifest, which are these; Adultery, fornication, uncleanness, lasciviousness, Idolatry, witchcraft, hatred, variance, emulations, wrath, strife, seditions, heresies, Envyings, murders, drunkenness, revellings, and such like: of the which I tell you before as

I have also told you in time past that they which do such things shall not inherit the kingdom of God. But the fruit of the Spirit is love, joy, peace, longsuffering, gentleness, goodness, faith, Meekness, temperance: against such there is no law. And they that are Christ's have crucified the flesh with the affections and lusts. If we live in the Spirit, let us also walk in the Spirit. **Galatians 5:18-25**

Jesus also said in this world we shall have tribulation, this is not our home. You cannot with one sorting out remove all the challenges of life. The answer is to live close to Jesus and learn to stand on the word by your-self. To tie everything to something in the past keeps you digging for sins under the blood of Jesus.

The tendency will be to return to issues and blame the past for the present. It is possible that some challenges may have roots in your history; if you needed prayer with this you must not become a prisoner of your past; you must not also become addicted to prayer for deliverance returning ever so often for the same process.

I learnt the value of standing on the word quite early as a spirit filled believer. As a young believer, I had some oppression during the night as I slept, all I did was to find scriptures that had to do with my authority in Christ, I meditated on them daily and prayed, all fears were gone, and when the attack came I was able to rebuke it and that was it.

I have never had that sort of oppression since then; I do not have fear of such oppression because I know my rights and privileges and have used my authority. If you constantly have to return to a man for your deliverance you remain a babe and you are easily subject to manipulation.

The best deliverance is to get in the word of God, stand on it and put Satan on the run (James 4:7). Every believer has same privileges and rights. Supposing you are in such a shape that you can't take up for yourself spiritually, then you need some help.

Get the help, the prayers you need but don't become a deliverance addict, I am aware of a case of someone who was always having something cast in and out until she became mentally afflicted and eventually died. To constantly run to some supposed spiritual therapy of deliverance on Christians by casting something in and casting something out of them is unscriptural. Jesus said in Mark 16:17 that all believers are to have authority over the enemy

"And when he was come to the other side into the country of the Gergesenes, there met him two possessed with devils, coming out of the tombs, exceeding fierce, so that no man might pass by that way.
And, behold, they cried out, saying, what have we to do with thee, Jesus, thou Son of God? Art thou come hither to torment us before the time? And there was a good way of from them an herd of many swine feeding.
So the devils besought him, saying, if thou cast us out, suffer us to go away into the herd of swine. And he said unto them, go. And when they were come out, they went into the herd of swine; and, behold, the whole herd of swine ran violently down a steep place into the sea, and perished in the waters.
And they that kept them fled, and went their ways into the city, and told everything, and what was befallen to the possessed of the

devils. And behold, the whole city came out to meet Jesus; and when they saw him, they sought him that he would depart out of their coasts". **MATTHEW 8:28-34**

Jesus did not spend his time recording demonic conversations and reading them to his disciples, in fact he had little interest in what the devil had to say.

The demon spoke out and asked Jesus if he had come to torment them before their time. This passage does not in any-way say Jesus tormented them. In fact, Jesus was only interested in setting the man free. Jesus defeated Satan on the cross.

Recording what demons have to say and reading it to the church is to believe a lie because Jesus said when Satan lies he speaks naturally. To confirm that some believers are evil or sinful because a demon said so during a time of deliverance is to abandon the word and chase shadows.

Imagine how much time people spend with the devil compared to how much time people spend in the word. Satan wants to keep people busy on the wrong thing, spending time unwisely. A day is coming when Satan will be sent to the lake of fire. Until that time he has a right to be around. Some waste useful time in tormenting the devil.

And Satan will definitely give people some weird manifestations which may convince them they are on track; people are hungry for the supernatural but are not discerning enough. Continuous focus on the devil makes people more devil conscious than word of God conscious. The intimate nature of some of the discussions and encounters has resulted in some ministers falling morally.

BLOOD OF SPRINKLING

"And Moses took the blood, and sprinkled it on the people, and said Behold the blood of the covenant, which the LORD hath made with you concerning all these words". **Exodus 24:8**

"And to Jesus the mediator of the new covenant, and to the blood of sprinkling, that speaketh better things than that of Abel". **HEBREWS 12:24.**

"And he took the cup, and gave thanks and gave it to them, saying Drink ye all of it; 28 For this is my blood of the new testament, which is shed for many for the remission of sins".
Matthew 26:27-28

"For when Moses had spoken every precept to all the people according to the law, he took the blood of calves and of goats, with water, and scarlet wool, and hyssop, and sprinkled both the book, and all the people, Saying This is the blood of the testament which God hath enjoined unto you.
Moreover, he sprinkled with blood both the tabernacle, and all the vessels of the ministry. And almost all things are by the law purged with blood; and without shedding of blood is no remission. It was therefore necessary that the patterns of things in the heavens should be purified with these; but the heavenly things themselves with better sacrifices than these.
For Christ is not entered into the holy places made with hands, which are the figures of the true; but into heaven itself, now to appear in the presence of God for us:
Nor yet that he should offer himself often, as the high priest entereth into the holy place every year with blood of others;

For then must he often have suffered since the foundation of the world: but now once in the end of the world hath he appeared to put away sin by the sacrifice of himself.
And as it is appointed unto men once to die but after this the judgment:
So Christ was once offered to bear the sins of many; and unto them that look for him shall he appear the second time without sin unto salvation. **Hebrews 9:19-28**

Blood of sprinkling is the practice of sprinkling Holy Communion on worshippers; we do not have new-testament precedence for this practice. In the old -testament Moses sprinkled the people after the covenant was ratified.

The communion table is an ordinance of the church that Jesus established himself, we cannot change it. Jesus commanded to eat the bread and drink of the cup he did not command us to sprinkle. Paul in the epistle said the same thing Jesus said. The revelation Paul had of the communion is the same as the one the apostles received. When Jesus appeared to Paul he did not give him a new ordinance neither can we. Hebrew 9:19-28 shows us that, Jesus actually went into heaven and sprinkled his blood over the altar as the final sacrifice.

No case can arise against the believer in heaven because Jesus already sprinkled the blood there and his sacrifice was accepted, the communion table is therefore a place where we come into agreement with God for all the things Jesus has done for our redemption.

It is a place of celebration of his death and resurrection. A place of appreciation and appropriating what he has done. The blood of Jesus has been sprinkled in heaven by Jesus your high priest for you, Old Testament priest sprinkled the blood on the earthly altar to make peace and entered the presence of God for the people; Jesus did it once and for all so you can have eternal peace to God. No pastor can sprinkle the blood on the altars of heaven for you there is only one High priest, his name is Jesus.

The passage above refers to what Jesus has done for us through his blood. By that blood we have received mercy; by that blood our lives have been changed. The blood has been sprinkled on the mercy seat of God as eternal evidence that you and I have been paid for in full. No accusation or evil has a right to come to us because of the blood.

These blessings can be appropriated by faith, and not by ceremonial sprinkling of people with communion wine. All you get is a wet shirt. It is faith based on the word of God in your heart that causes you to appropriate the blessing.

It is true that the Old Testament records people being sprinkled in Lev. 14:7, Lev 16:14, and so on.

We must remember that God worked with the Old Testament saints from the outside to the inside because they were not saved people, God couldn't live in them. In fact God's presence dwelt in the tabernacle. In the New Testament Jesus lives in our hearts by the Holy Spirit. The blood of Jesus is already sprinkled, when Jesus our high priest appeared in the altar of God in heaven and we can appropriate the benefits when we come to the communion table.

It is impossible for any human being to get to the altar in heaven and sprinkle that blood, old testament priest had an earthly altar, which they approached by the blood of animals, Jesus entered the heavenly tabernacle after he paid with his own blood, he sprinkled that blood once and for all to make eternal peace for us and guarantee all the benefits of salvation.

In the Old Testament, the blood was sprinkled on their bodies in the New Testament we appropriate the blessings of the blood through our confession.

FEET WASHING

"Jesus knowing that the Father had given all things into his hands, and that he was come from God, and went to God; He riseth from supper, and laid aside his garments; and took a towel, and girded himself. After that he poureth water into a bason, and began to wash the disciples' feet, and to wipe them with the towel wherewith he was girded. Then cometh he to Simon Peter: and Peter saith unto him, Lord, dost thou wash my feet?
Jesus answered and said unto him, What I do thou knowest not now; but thou shalt know hereafter. Peter saith unto him, Thou shalt never wash my feet. Jesus answered him, If I

wash thee not, thou hast no part with me. Simon Peter saith unto him, Lord, not my feet only, but also my hands and my head.

Jesus saith to him, He that is washed needeth not save to wash his feet, but is clean every whit: and ye are clean, but not all.

For he knew who should betray him; therefore said he Ye are not all clean. So after he had washed their feet, and had taken his garments, and was set down again, he said unto them, Know ye what I have done to you?

Ye call me Master and Lord: and ye say well; for so I am. If I then, your Lord and Master, have washed your feet; ye also ought to wash one another's feet. For I have given you an example, that ye should do as I have done to you. Verily, verily, I say unto you, The servant is not greater than his lord; neither he that is sent greater than he that sent him. **JOHN 13:3-16**

The incident of washing of feet is recorded once in the ministry of Jesus, that he washed his disciples' feet as a symbol of humility and to show them an example of how they ought to serve one another. (John 13:5-14).

There are other examples of washing found in the Old Testament Lev 6:27, Lev 14:9, Lev 15:16, Ex 29:4, Deut 21:6, Gen 18:4, Gen 24:32, Gen 43:24, and so on".

Old Testament people were not capable of spirit-led righteous-living and therefore the Lord allowed them outside holiness rather than inward holiness, as a result of which there were so many ceremonial washings. Before the scribes wrote the name of God they even took a ritual bath as a sign of reverence to the Lord. In the New Testament we are cleansed by the washing of water by the word (Eph 5:26).

The reason given by some to wash feet is to make the people holy, so that their feet do not slip into evil places. What has happened to the blood of Jesus (1 Jn 1:9)? Without the word working in a man's heart, he could bathe in the ocean and still be live unholy.

Some use it as a key to success and prosperity. Prospering in God comes by consistent and diligent walk with God, and the laws that govern prosperity in the Bible.

A symbolic washing of feet does not translate to abundance, if one has received a prophetic word in this direction and had results by washing feet this cannot be made into a New Testament doctrine, where breakthroughs service come through washing the feet.

Jesus washed the disciples' feet to teach them humility, they had been walking on muddy roads with animal waste and Jesus washed their feet, a job normally reserved for servants in a household when visitors arrived.

He asked them to serve one another. There is no New Testament basis for washing people's feet to become wealthy.

WAR TONGUES
"Follow after charity, and desire spiritual gifts, but rather that ye may prophesy. For he that speaketh in an unknown tongue speaketh not unto men, but unto God: for no man understandeth him; howbeit in the spirit he speaketh mysteries. But he that prophesieth speaketh unto men to edification, and exhortation, and comfort. He that speaketh in an unknown tongue edifieth himself; but he that prophesieth edifieth the church.

I would that ye all spake with tongues, but rather that ye prophesied for greater is he that prophesieth than he that speaketh with tongues, except he interpret that the church may receive edifying. **1 Corinthians 14:1-5**

"For the weapons of our warfare are not carnal, but mighty through God to the pulling down of strong holds; Casting down imaginations, and every high thing that exalteth itself against the knowledge of God, and bringing into captivity every thought to the obedience of Christ". **2 Corinthians 10**

It is believed that there is a special tongue with which you speak to Satan. The fact that a tongue sounds aggressive does not make it a war tongue except the spirit of God reveals that to you.

What he reveals to you may not be revealed to others. They may end up concocting something and call it war tongues. If the Holy Spirit does not show you the interpretation of your words in tongues you cannot know the meaning.

The scripture teaches that tongues is primarily a devotional gift for fellowshipping with the father and secondarily used in prophetic utterance to bless the body but you cannot find a scripture saying we should use our tongues to speak to Satan. An experience where a believer feels this has happened cannot be made into a doctrine where everyone wants to identify the tongues used to speak to the devil because without interpretation or revelation you cannot understand what you are saying in tongues. All the gifts operate as the spirit of God wills so you cannot determine this and ask everybody to do the same.

The 'least' of believers has authority to rebuke the devil, cast him out without praying in tongues. You need the word of God and your authority not a special tongue to cast out devil. What is the use in conversing with the devil who Jesus calls a liar?

The Bible plainly teaches that when we speak in tongues we speak to God and we edify ourselves. But some argue that they feel good when they use their tongues to speak to the devil.

The simple truth is that if you pray in tongues the Bible says you will be edified, that explains the good feeling. This ditch is creating serious problem for genuine seekers of the Holy Ghost baptism; people are seeking to enrich their prayer life with God and not having conversation with Satan. The question I like to ask those who war against Satan in tongues is: how do they get their reply from Satan during their conversation?

Satan is a liar (John 8:44); the Bible says he is the father of lies. Holding conversation with a liar is unprofitable when you have the truth of God's word (Jn. 17:17).

The extreme practice of travelling to specific locations and arising at midnight to fight against some spirits, or even going into a river to do warfare cannot be made into a doctrine. God may lead believers to do certain prophetic things but you cannot turn this into a church doctrine.

Daniel did not realize the tremendous spiritual opposition against him until the angel revealed it. He also did not need to travel to the kingdom where the resistance took place to be effective. There is no distance in the spirit, your words and authority will work anywhere in heaven on earth and under the earth. Prophetic directions must not be made into a new doctrine.

The scripture teaches that tongues is primarily a devotional gift for fellowshipping with the father and secondarily used in prophetic utterance to bless the body but you cannot find a scripture saying we should use our tongues to speak to Satan. (Daniel 10:11-13)

The scripture teaches that tongues is primarily a devotional gift for fellowshipping with the father and secondarily used in prophetic utterance to bless the body but you cannot find a scripture saying we should use our tongues to speak to Satan.

GROANING AT WILL

"Likewise the spirit also helpeth our infirmities for we know not what we should pray for as we ought: but the spirit itself maketh intercession for us with groaning which cannot be uttered. And he that searcheth the hearts knoweth what is the mind of the Spirit, because he

maketh intercession for the saints according to the will of God. **ROMANS 8:26-27**

."Who hath heard such a thing? Who hath seen such things? Shall the earth be made to bring forth in one day? Or shall a nation be born at once? For as soon as Zion travailed, she brought forth her children". **ISAIAH 66:8**

It is true that sometimes in intercessory prayer, the spirit begins to give us groaning and as we express them, victory comes. But on the other hand, some teach that you groan at will whenever you want to. The Bible likens this manifestation of the spirit to a woman in labor (Is. 66:8) A woman in labor only travails when the time for the delivery comes.

She does not make it up. The teaching on groaning-at-will is erroneous because the Bible teaches that the spirit HELPETH. We don't do it without the spirit's help, without labor pains a woman cannot groan. We cannot generate the energy of the spirit in the flesh. The eagle rides the current but cannot glide when there is no current, a person wind surfing cannot surf without the waves.

Some kind of spiritual acrobatics in the flesh no matter how spectacular have no power. A woman never has a baby in public. Much of the groaning seen in some places are public, rolling on the ground, aching, screaming like a woman in labor puts the attention on the person praying.

Some of these encounters should be precious times in private, no sane woman wants to have her baby in the public glare. On the other hand, it does not rule out the real groaning through the spirit.

All spirit filled believers must be open and indeed count it an honor when the Lord calls them to this kind of intercession. Some today are completely scared, yet the spirit may be willing at times to give such manifestations.
Groaning led by the spirit of God allows us to birth things in the spirit; life and death situations may be changed by spirit led groaning. Groaning by the Holy Spirit is scriptural. When the burden lifts you know you are done and peace returns, you are not groaning based on a register like every three hours groan, this is flesh driven. You cannot

set up a groaning roaster by the Spirit, he determines when there is a need for it.

MAJOR ON MAJOR

"Now the Spirit speaketh expressly that in the later times some shall depart from the faith, giving heed to seducing spirit, and doctrines of the devil; Speaking lies in hypocrisy; having their conscience seared with a hot iron".
1TIMOTHY 4:1-2

"Quench not the Spirit. Despise not prophesyings. Prove all things; hold fast that which is good. Abstain from all appearance of evil. And the very God of peace sanctify you wholly; and I pray God your whole spirit and soul and body be preserved blameless unto the coming of our Lord Jesus Christ. Faithful is he that calleth you, who also will do it. **1 Thessalonians 5: 19-24**

Nahab and Abihu offered strange fire and got killed. They did things their own way. You cannot do it your own way for so long without getting into trouble. We are grateful for the mercy of God when we are ignorant God winks at this but when we deceitfully handle the word for pecuniary reasons we are in danger of judgment.

It is difficult to know the motive of a man's heart, but we can look at the fruit of his ministry, we can also look at the word of God to see what the word says about what doctrine or revelation is being preached.

One of the signs of the end time is that people will depart from the faith (1 Tim 4:1-2). He did not say they will reject the Lord outright but that they will depart from sound teaching.

They will still profess to be believers. The early church confronted the crisis of doctrinal extremes vigorously. Today extreme teachings and demonic doctrines have engulfed some of the body of Christ. Jude warns (Jude verse 3-4), saying we should earnestly contend for the faith. To contend is to defend the truth. It is important to note that the people spreading falsehood here were brethren, not unbelievers.

When one speaks about dangerous extremes people are quick to warn you about love, but the Bible says love rejoices in truth only. Was

Paul walking in love in (Acts 20:28)? Was Paul walking in love when he even mentioned by name Hymenaeus Alexander (I Tim 1:20) and warned people about them? What about (2 Tim 2:16)?

What about Demas (Tim 4:10)? Paul revealed his backsliding. Was Apostle John walking in love when he warned the church about Diotrephes (3 John 9 and 10)? Was Peter walking in love when he warned about false prophets and teachers (2 Pet 2:1-3) (2 Pet 2:12)?

Let us take a sampling of some of these scriptures:

"Take heed therefore unto yourselves, and to all the flock, over the which the Holy Ghost hath made you overseers, to feed the church of God, which he hath purchased with his own blood. For I know this, that after my departing shall grievous wolves enter in among you, not sparing the flock. Also of your own selves shall men arise speaking perverse things to draw away disciples after them. Therefore watch and remember that by the space of three years

I ceased not to warn every one night and day with tears". **Acts 20:28-31**

" This charge I commit unto thee, son Timothy, according to the prophecies which went before on thee, that thou by them mightest war a good warfare; Holding faith, and a good conscience; which some having put away concerning faith have made shipwreck. Of whom is Hymenaeus and Alexander; whom I have delivered unto Satan, that they may learn not to blaspheme. **2 Timothy 2:16-17**

"But shun profane and vain babblings: for they will increase unto more ungodliness. And their word will eat as doth a canker: of whom is Hymenaeus and Philetus; **1 Timothy 1:18-20**

"But there were false prophets also among the people, even as there shall be false teachers among you, who privily shall bring in damnable heresies, even denying the Lord that bought them, and bring upon themselves swift destruction. And many shall follow their pernicious ways; by reason of whom the way of truth shall be evil spoken of. And through covetousness shall they with feigned words make merchandise of you: whose judgment

now of a long time lingereth not, and their damnation slumbereth not". **2 Peter 2:1-3**

"But these, as natural brute beasts, made to be taken and destroyed, speak evil of the things that they understand not and shall utterly perish in their own corruption; And shall receive the reward of unrighteousness, as they that count it pleasure to riot in the day time. Spots they are and blemishes, sporting themselves with their own deceivings while they feast with you; Having eyes full of adultery, and that cannot cease from sin; beguiling unstable souls: an heart they have exercised with covetous practices; cursed children:

Which have forsaken the right way, and are gone astray following the way of Balaam the son of Bosor, who loved the wages of unrighteousness;

But was rebuked for his iniquity: the dumb ass speaking with man's voice forbad the madness of the prophet. These are wells without water, clouds that are carried with a tempest; to whom the mist of darkness is reserved for ever.

For when they speak great swelling words of vanity, they allure through the lusts of the flesh, through much wantonness, those that were clean escaped from them who live in error. While they promise them liberty, they themselves are the servants of corruption: for of whom a man is overcome of the same is he brought in bondage

For if after they have escaped the pollutions of the world through the knowledge of the Lord and Saviour Jesus Christ, they are again entangled therein, and overcome the latter end is worse with them than the beginning. For it had been better for them not to have known the way of righteousness, than, after they have known it, to turn from the holy commandment delivered unto them.

But it is happened unto them according to the true proverb, The dog is turned to his own vomit again and the sow that was washed to her wallowing in the mire. **2 Peter 2:12-22**

The truth is that love wants to warn of danger to protect the body. Today the devil is determined to slow the move of God down or pervert it with counterfeit, so-called new manifestation that are grossly unscriptural.

On the other hand those unscriptural extremes should not make us run from genuine move of

God (1 Thes 5:19-20). "Prove all things but don't quench the spirit."

Some however want to major in the minor or in other words have a whirlwind in a teacup. There are several things we must wink at because they don't amount to much anyway. But there are other things that need to be corrected otherwise deception will be the order of the day. No long ago, an occultist simply changed the signboard of his church to that of a gospel church and carried on as usual because there was no real difference between how he operated and the gospel church.

There is no substitute for a consistent, devotional spirit led faith walk with God. People are told if you are sick use olive oil, if you need money use olive oil. This has become a substitute for the word. In Matthew 4:4 Jesus said, "Man shall not live by bread alone but by every word of God."

When signs become the goal of the believer, instead of producing signs and allowing our lives to become living letters the believer runs aimlessly. The more Christ-like we become, we are not tossed to and fro, we know him for ourselves.

Paul's quest was to know God to be intimate with him; he was also prepared to suffer for his beliefs. In the age of quick fixes the natural or carnal believer does not care if his result comes through the word of God or any other way.

EXTREME DISCIPLESHIP

"Go ye therefore, and teach all nations, baptizing them in the name of the Father, and of the Son, and of the Holy Ghost: Teaching them to observe all things whatsoever I have commanded you: and, lo I am with you always, even unto the end of the world. Amen". **Matthew 28:19-20**

"And the things that thou hast heard of me among many witnesses, the same commit thou to faithful men, who shall be able to teach others also". **2 Timothy2:2**

The command to go and make disciples is a command from the Lord Jesus. Discipleship is central to the growth of the believer and fulfillment of the church that we cannot shy away from the assignment irrespective of extremes.

The discipleship ensures that the crowd becomes an army, the converts become believers and are not constantly converting to something else. The Lord Jesus employed the same method in training his disciples. He mentored them.

The word disciple means a disciplined follower, discipleship turns a convert into a mature believer, it is the act of mentoring a younger believer to become a real follower. He learns by precepts and example, during the period of training a relationship develops as the new believer is mentored, the challenge comes when this degenerate to control of every area of the new believer's life. Discipleship is to turn the attention of the younger believer to Christ, helping them to learn more about Christ.

The new believer should be learning dependency on God, hearing the voice of God, developing character. When the new believer cannot make any personal decisions, and has to depend on the mentor for the intimate decisions of his marriage and is duty bound to obey his mentor even when it violates his conscience it becomes an abuse. People have been known to work without pay, given up valuables at the instance of their mentor or discipleship leader, only to cry in secret.

The training of an eagle which can be likened to the training the believer goes through is a process to make the eaglet skilled and mature enough to survive in the wild. When a discipleship leader has all his followers tied to him for the most basic decisions, he is not training them to be fruitful. The new disciple should be strong enough to look after others in the body.

CHAPTER 2

FAITH, A WAY OF LIFE

One of the reasons fetishes and short cuts have risen is that faith is not a way of life but a means to solve problems.

"But without faith it is impossible to please him: for he that cometh to God must believe that he is, and he is a rewarder of them that diligently seek him". **HEBREWS11:6**

"So then faith cometh by hearing, and hearing by the word of God". **ROMANS 10:17**

Looking unto Jesus the author and finisher of our faith; who for the joy that was set before him endured the cross, despising the shame, and is set down at the right hand of the throne of God. **HEBREWS 12:2.**

"The sower soweth the word. And these are they by the way side, where the word is sown but when they have heard Satan cometh immediately, and taketh away the word that was sown in their hearts. And these are they likewise which are sown on stony ground; who, when they have heard the word, immediately receive it with gladness; And have no root in themselves, and so endure but for a time: afterward, when affliction or persecution ariseth for the word's sake, immediately they are offended And these are they which are sown among thorns; such as hear the word, And the cares of this world, and the deceitfulness of riches, and the lusts of other things entering in choke the word, and it becometh unfruitful. And he said So is the kingdom of God, as if a man should cast seed into the ground;
And should sleep and rise night and day, and the seed should spring and grow up he knoweth not how. For the earth bringeth forth fruit of herself; first the blade, then the ear, after that the full corn in the ear. But when the

fruit is brought forth immediately he putteth in the sickle, because the harvest is come". **MARK 4:14-19,26-29.**

"And I say also unto thee, that thou art Peter, and upon this rock I will build my church; and the gates of hell shall not prevail against it ". **MATTHEW 16:18**

"For verily I say unto you, that whosoever shall say unto this mountain, be thou removed, and be thou cast into the sea; and shall not doubt in his heart, but shall believe that those things which he saith shall come to pass; he shall have whatsoever he saith. Therefore I say unto you, what things soever ye desire, when ye pray, believe that ye receive them and ye shall have them". **MARK 11:23-24**

When some hear for the first time all the possibilities and blessings that can come to them when they live by faith, they are excited and ready to walk by faith but when troubles arise, disappointments or delays they are ready to quit. This is partly responsible for all the quick, short cuts people result to they desire results.

Jesus taught that for the word to really work and produce fruit it takes time. In fact Jesus likens the walk of faith to that of a farmer, one who sows seeds. A farmer is thinking of sowing seeds, weeding, watering, pruning, harvesting, preparing the ground for the next planting and the circle goes on and on.

The farmer's life revolves around the farm, the soil, the seed. Those who have been disappointed trying to walk by faith are usually those who allow tests, trials, persecution, lack of commitment to the word or using the word as a spare tire to defeat them.

Bad experiences do not change the truth of God's word. A farmer lives and thinks farming, it is not a fad, it is not a flash in the pan, he is not trying out something new. It is not an option but a way of life. Some have seen faith as something you use in time of trouble but God does not see it that way.

The Just shall live by faith (Heb.l0:38), or we can rephrase it and say "The just shall live by breathing faith air". You can't live without breathing. Parents do not remind their children to remember to breathe because it is normal.

Breathing is not a movement, it is not a fad, it is not activity we engage in when in danger, it is our life. If we stop breathing we die.

God expects faith to be a normal way for us. We are called believers because we are, and we have the capacity of God to believe. Faith is simply believing and acting on what God says.

Romans 12:3 says every believer has been given the measure of faith, which means the capacity to believe is in you. As you hear the word of God and that word enters your heart the faith of God in your heart rises. For the purpose of illustration, if we liken the faith in the heart to a balloon, how much air the balloon gets determines how well the balloon would lift up. The word is the air that inflates the balloon.

It is important to note that God has given you his ability to believe (Heb. 12:2). The faith of God in you is not weak. So many times it takes time for the word to pass through all the traditions and past thinking in the mind before it can come into the heart or spirit and then illumination comes.

That is the time people can boldly act on the word of God. Jesus said, the church is built on this type of knowledge - he calls it a rock (Matt. 16:18). It is the type of knowledge no one can take away from you. It is not presumptuous. Heart faith produces quiet assurance in the face of the storm. (Isaiah 30:15)

You know that you know. This is a knowledge that comes from God's spirit to yours. It can be revealed by the Holy Spirit when you meditate on the word. It takes time for the balloon to get enough air before it can lift, when the balloon has enough air it lifts without a struggle.

It takes time of meditating (Josh. 1:8, Col 3:16-17) and confessing those truths. Those looking for quick fixes are not patient enough before the harvest is ready they try to manufacture something and fall flat. Unfortunately some who trust God for one thing or the other jump out before they are ready.

THE WORD MUST WORK IN YOU BEFORE WORKING THROUGH YOU. Some believers hear a man who has spent many years in some scriptures on a certain thing and they copy and fail and then wonder why in the process they create a scandal.

If you want to work in faith in any area of your life, let the word of God become a way of life, and then be patient. You can't go beyond the light you have in your heart Jesus said in Mark 4:26-29 the farmer plants the seed, he is patient, he waters and that seed keeps working in the soil which is a type of the heart.

The word of God you hear is the seed. A good farmer is diligently watering, weeding, and being patient; then comes the blade, the ear, the full corn, and then the harvest. Because you have the capacity to believe like God, if you just get the seed (the word) into that soil, it will produce; but many are seeking the harvest before the word even settles in those areas, and so no harvest comes.

Your heart, the soil, is designed to receive the seed of God's word; when the word takes root, it sprouts and produces harvest with

PATIENCE.
Differentiating Between Special Manifestations and Standing for Yourself. You

can come into some of our meetings and see many instant healings, people removing hearing aids, cripple walking, blind eyes seeing, deaf hearing and so on. The truth in most cases is that these moves of God are special manifestations of the Spirit, God's gift of faith is usually in manifestation and the person used by God in these situations knows he is operating under a greater grace and things happen as people also respond in faith. He may not be able to reproduce the same feat one hour after once the anointing lifts.

There is a world of difference when the Holy Ghost is in manifestation and when you are walking in faith by yourself in your home; it is like taking a plane and driving a car. One goes much quicker. Some have thrown their glasses away just because somebody else did so.

Where there is no special move of the Holy Ghost you need to stay in the word and begin to act upon it as you gain more light. When you are standing in the word you don't need someone to tell you when the word has really settled in you. A pregnant woman knows she is pregnant. A believer who is really "pregnant" with the word can confidently act on the word to the level of the word he has digested.

God does not honor copying others but his word. Some close down their Bank account because some prophet told them to do so. Again, you don't get anything back if it was not a special manifestation of God confirmed by the Holy Spirit to you or acting based on the word and the inspiration of the Holy Spirit.

The widow of Zerephath in 1 kings obeyed a prophetic word and was blessed, the boy who gave Jesus his lunch fed five thousand people in response to a divine request and was blessed. The New Testament believer has a responsibility to be led by the Holy Spirit, you need to have confirmation in your heart and when you do the blessings of God will be there.

I remember in a meeting where I prayed for a woman who got out of the wheelchair without my realizing it, because I had my eyes closed. When people began to scream I opened my eyes and saw she was walking. In the same meeting, another woman didn't get out of her chair. I was wondering what to do as the first healing was rather dramatic, but the Lord spoke to me to give her all the healing scriptures I knew and encourage her to think on them daily. To the glory of God, fear left her; she grew stronger and got out of that chair. The following year she was also out of the chair. The word lodged in her heart and she knew she was healed and finally the healing manifested, according to her testimony she was 'healed' before she was 'healed'.

When you are standing in faith by yourself you would know that you have the answer before anything happens physically. Why? The word of God in your heart brings this realization. That is HEART FAITH not HEAD FAITH. Mark 11:23 says if you believe with your heart not your head...

To believe with the heart comes by revelation of God's word in a man's heart. It takes time for food to digest and, similarly, it is only the food you digest that gives energy. It takes diligence for the word to go from the head to the heart.

If you take the word according to Joshua 1:8 and you meditate on it, it would first change your thinking (3John 2), (Rom. 12:2), (Prov.

4:20-22) and eventually it will enter your heart. When this happens, God's faith which he gave you when you receive Jesus (Rom 12:3) will begin to get built up or inflated like a balloon.

On your own you'd discover that you act on the word boldly. An inflated balloon lifts up without struggle. If you think on the word prayerfully until it enters into your heart you will know you are healed, your needs are met even before they happen in the physical because the word has entered into your heart.

Jesus said in Mark 4 that when the seed is planted and watered it grows first the blade, the corn in the ear and the full corn, then the harvest.

You cannot reap before harvest time. Many hear a scripture once and they want a harvest 'yesterday'. They fail; but God has not failed. The word in your heart therefore becomes the evidence of what you want from God.

It becomes your spiritual substance (Heb 11:1). You cannot see the answer physically but you have the answer in your heart through the word. That assurance is what prompts you to act, not copying someone's experience.

Receiving the Word in Your Heart
Let us understand that anything human beings are involved with would be prone to mistakes because human beings are not perfect. To throw away the principle God himself lives by is to open the door for deception.

Human errors do not make bible truths invalid. The Bible says God formed the world by faith - filled - words and He calls those "things which be not as though they were "(Rom 4:17).

God authored faith. Faith is a way of life and walking by faith and not by feelings should be in every area of life and not just in one. Some only want to use their faith to get money not to live a holy life.
It takes faith to work in holiness and the fruit of the spirit because when your body wants to sin you must believe you are saved when your body doesn't feel that is true.

I.   Meditate the word (Josh 1:8, Prov. 4:20-22)
II.   Give thanks continually (Ps. 50:23)

III.   Act on the Word (James 2:20)

IV.   Patiently expect results (James 1)

Unbelief of others should not deter us from walking in what Jesus has provided. The unbelief of some should not make our faith ineffective.

Preaching unbelief, trying very hard to avoid the mention of faith is not the answer. God has ordained that the principle of faith be an essential part of everyday living. If you don't walk in faith you'd walk in fear. Romans 3:3-4

Fear brings Satan on the scene; faith brings God on the scene. You cannot receive righteousness, holiness, healing, and fruit of the spirit or receive salvation for your beloved ones, physical provisions and so on without faith. Why? When your feelings don't agree that you are saved you need the word in your heart. To refuse to preach faith to God's people is to close the door of real intimacy with God.

We don't see God physically to get close to Him, and so we must believe His word. This is one reason for the so many depressed believers we have today. They are trying to contact God with their feelings outside of his word. Unbelief brings death, faith brings life and freedom.

One of the reasons many new believers are unable to take up for themselves is because they believe that those who are used of God are far better than them and have a better access to God.

A minister may have gifts operating in them, and by reason of use have exercised and developed intimacy with God but every believer can learn to flow in the Holy Spirit.

God is calling all of us to come boldly the throne of grace, he is calling us to come boldly, this is not arrogance, no one is going on his own credit we all approach based on the redemption through the blood of Jesus. The father wants us to come and worship not only making request but just being intimate with him.

Any believer can meditate the word and apply to their lives, when the minister insists that his revelations are so deep and full of mysteries specially revealed to him, the average believer has no choice than to wait on him to dissect the mysteries if he chooses.

The word of God is simple and needs to be preached with simplicity; Jesus used what people could relate to in expressing deep truths. A revelation that is so deep that most of the church cannot understand is suspect. A revelation so deep only ties people to the apron of the minister not the word of God

"Seeing then that we have a great high priest, that is passed into the heavens, Jesus the Son of God, let us hold fast our profession. For we have not an high priest which cannot be touched with the feeling of our infirmities; but was in all points tempted like as we are, yet without sin. Let us therefore come boldly unto the throne of grace, that we may obtain mercy, and find grace to help in time of need". **Hebrews 4:14-16**

"For he hath made him to be sin for us, who knew no sin; that we might be made the righteousness of God in him". **2CORINTHIANS 5:21**

"Herein is our love made perfect, that we may have boldness in the Day of Judgment: because as he is, so are we in this world". **1JOHN 4:17**

"For we are his workmanship, created in Christ Jesus unto good works, which God hath before ordained that we should walk in them". **EPHESIANS 2:10**

"I, even I am he that bloteth out thy transgressions for mine own sake, and will not remember thy sins". **ISAIAH 43:25.**

"Whereby are given unto us exceeding great and precious promises: that by these ye might be partakers of the divine nature, having escaped the corruption that is in the world through lust". **2 Peter 1:4**

It is not pride to go before the Lord with boldness, to call yourself redeemed, righteous, healed, delivered, and blessed because you are.

All curses were broken when Jesus went to the cross. One reason some are always looking for the latest sign or the latest prophet is the sense of unworthiness and fear to approach God on their own.

They become easy targets for charlatans and fly by night ministers. A case in point was a minister who told a certain married woman to come to his hotel for prayers; he succeeded in taking advantage of her and defiling her and even tried to break up her marriage.

False Humility

It is very difficult to walk in a straight line. No wonder the Bible says broad is the way that leads to destruction, because it's much easier to branch off than to walk the narrow way.

The ditch of "don't-think-you -are -anything' is an attempt by human flesh to keep people humble. Feelings of unworthiness do not change the fact that God has blotted all our sins and put his nature of righteousness, it is a gift we cannot work for it. Romans 5:17.

It is harmful to deny the accomplishments of Jesus in our behalf in the name of false humility. People are constantly encouraged to feel they are not good enough, "Don't say anything good about yourself, keep everybody on the same level", it pleases the flesh but displeases the spirit.

God never made us in uniform. The human fingers are not equal but each has a unique function and so you can't cut them to the same size, so also it is in the body of Christ.

This teaching or attitude is contrary to the fact that we are new creations (Eph 2:10, 2 Cor. 5:21). God did not make any weak new creation. God has completely wiped out our past (Is. 43:25). No past for the believers. When a new child is born he is seen as innocent and pure, God sees us the same way.

The Bible teaches that we are joint heirs with Christ (Eph 2) seated with him (2 Pet. 1:4) and that we are partakers of God's nature (Acts 1:8) filled with the same spirit as Jesus (Rom 8:11). We are to come boldly to the throne of God.

It is not who we are in the flesh but whose we are that counts (Acts 27:23; 1 John 4:4). We are of God and he chooses to name us after himself. Everything God calls us emanates from his character. A man may buy a dog and call him Jack or George, the dog has a right to that name and needs no apologies because the owner named him. Christ.

As Jesus is, so are we now. The Bible says we have the same nature (1 Jn. 4:17). The devil is out there accusing' the Christians of all his faults and past life. This combined with the teaching, 'You are no good" 'You are nothing" "You are not worthy" simply places the believer in a place of defeat, doubt and fear. God says he is in us now.

Romans 5:17, says that righteousness is a gift of God as a result of Jesus' sacrifice; it is not humility to refuse to accept the fullness of Jesus' sacrifice. He calls you righteous, beloved, saint, friend, joint heir, light, temple of God, and "don't think you are anything".

There is sometimes an attempt to pull down anyone who tries to stand for God or for anything. This only leads to mediocrity, living in bondage to a system where you cannot aspire for excellence.

God has put different abilities in every believer as we rise up in resurrection power with the fruit of the spirit we can walk in God's fullness and still be humble. A man who tries to impress you with his humility is really proud of his humility and it is still pride. God created us to show forth his glory. Imagine your son coming home and he informs you that his teacher said: "I wonder who you are, you look like a monkey.

I wonder who your parents are, I don't think you are anything" you will be unhappy. People tell many lies on God's new creation. God has created you in His image; don't let anyone create you into their image.

In the eyes of God, you look like Jesus, not because of who you are in the flesh but because of the work of substitution Jesus did on the cross. Jesus took your place on the cross that you may stand in the presence of God.

Many times, the need to cut others down is actually a manifestation of our own fear of being dominated by others. The secret is to find your gift and be your best at it. It is not so important how many talents you have but your faithfulness with what you have been given.

'Don't-think-you-are-anything' mentality leads to fear, criticism and silent competition. People are constantly afraid to do anything for God because someone thinks they are proud and would criticize them. It is like a dog in a manger, what you can't get you destroy. This spirit is demonic and has killed and is killing many a revival.

It is a controlling spirit; it attempts to keep everything in and everybody in check. History has shown that whenever believers bring set laws to control everyone the move of God is stifled.

This poor image created about the believer makes some believe they can't trust God for anything. The emphasis on the minister's words and revelations can go too far and many can tell you what their pastor, prophet, apostle, bishop and others said but they cannot tell you what the word said to them today or what the Holy Spirit is saying to them now. They are so ministers or pastor dependent that after many years the most basic things cannot be done except they see their pastor. This is a church filled with babies and is a spiritual nursery at best.

Believers should not feel like orphans and worms, if they do their faith will be weakened and will continually depend on their ministers and others for the most basic needs. To continually say you cannot, you are nothing, you are unable, is to put your faith in the flesh and not in the finished work.

God has said good things about you. He has called us here are a few samples: "Partakers of the divine nature" (2 Pet 1:4) "Sons of God" (John. 1:12)   "Light of the World" (Matt 5:14)   "Ambassadors" (2 Cor 5:20)   "Righteousness" (2 Cor 5:21) "Saint" (Rom 1:7) "Joint Heir" (Rom 8:17) "Friend" (John. 15:14) "Apple of God's eyes" (Zech 2:8) "Salt" (Matt 5:13)

Seeing us through the shed blood of Jesus, God sees his own children carrying the same life. In his eyes you look like him in the spirit, because like begets like. A lioness doesn't give birth to a piglet and vice versa. All the muscles and bones a baby needs are present at birth if they are healthy, the new creation is healthy, God sees you as himself all you need is grow and come to fullness, he did not make one kind of new creation when he made pastors and another type when he made other believers.

The new creation is the same but the gifts and callings are different. On the other hand, I have met those who do not believe in pastors or ministers. Jesus was clear that he has given gifts to men and they are equipped to stand in those offices. They are called to perfect the saints, help the saints become more mature that they are able to do the work of the ministry. Ephesians 4:11-12

The goal of the ministry gifts is to help the believers to be matured so believers are actively involved in ministering to the lost and helping others to find wholeness.

A day is coming when the church will arise as a mighty army, the ministers will continue to train the church but great signs and wonders will begin to happen in through believers it will be the day of great church. In our church over the years some women have testified to raising the dead as well as other small groups of believers in the church.
If you do not know your authority, rights and privileges, you won't be ready when the Lord

leads you into this type of adventures because your vision is yourself and your own problem. In a tunneled vision you see only one person himself.

CHAPTER 3

SPIRIT OF POVERTY

Christ hath redeemed us from the curse of the law, being made a curse for us: for it is written, cursed is everyone that hangeth on a tree.
GALATIANS 3:13

But thou shalt remember the Lord thy God: for it is he that giveth thee power to get wealth, that he may establish his covenant which he sware unto thy fathers, as it is this day.
DEUTERONOMY 8:18

Instances of strange fires seem to be motivated by need for finances, the need for money should not degenerate into love of money. It is important to consider the spirit of poverty in the last days because we must be careful not to fall in the ditch on either side. Some people believe poverty is a virtue, to others poverty is only found in war ravaged countries, and places with famine. But a close look at the Bible shows that the spirit of poverty is part of the curse of the law that Jesus redeemed us from.

Poverty is well and alive everywhere, material abundance is not necessarily a manifestation of God's prosperity. Redemption from the curse means God has given us empowerment to move forward and meet every need in life be it spiritual, emotional, material, financial, social and every area of human endeavor because the Bible says the gospel is the power of God to change anything.

The covenant of blessing as seen in the life of Abraham showed that although Abraham left home, God took care of him in a foreign land and he prospered. When because of fear he lied that his wife was his sister God turned the situation around and favored him. Isaac was also in a foreign land when a famine was on he was able to sow and reap a hundredfold.

He increased until his enemies came to celebrate him and made peace with him. It was all a manifestation of the covenant of blessing not his smartness.

Jacob his son, although driven from home because of a misdeed ended up blessed of God, he left with a stick and twenty years later he was blessed of God, this was not due to favorable working conditions or appreciation from his boss it was a great favor for the Lord.

Through the sacrifice of Jesus, we have been redeemed from all curses including poverty, we are the seed of Abraham through Christ therefore the blessing of Abraham is ours and much more because we operate under a better covenant.

The covenant that Jesus made with the father in our behalf is curse free because Jesus took all curses that were to come if we failed, as the high priest and advocate of this covenant he made peace in heaven for us.

"Christ hath redeemed us from the curse of the law, being made a curse for us: for it is written Cursed is everyone that hangeth on a tree: That the blessing of Abraham might come on

the Gentiles through Jesus Christ; that we might receive the promise of the Spirit through faith". **Galatians 3:13-14**

Poverty is a curse and it is a spirit. It is not measured by the size of the bank account. The spirit of poverty is closely related to the spirit of lack, shortage, and fear of losing what you have. Jesus came that we may have abundant life free of fear, confident that our heavenly father is more than sufficient.

"The thief cometh but to steal, and to kill, and to destroy: I am come that they might have life and that they might have it more abundantly". **John 10:10**

The spirit of poverty can be seen in the life of a man with millions of dollars in his bank account, as well as in a man who doesn't have a dollar to his name living in the worst ghetto of the world. Through the Old Testament and New Testament God has always-intended to be the source for his people. He told Abraham in Gen 12:1-3 that he would bless him and make him a blessing. He told the patriarchs Isaac and Jacob, the same thing, as well as their descendants.

In the New Testament, the Bible declares that Jesus became a curse for us. Poverty was a curse in the Old Testament. The problem is that many people do not recognize the spirit of poverty because the message of prosperity has been misused by some, but that does not make it untrue.

"Christ hath redeemed us from the curse of the law being made a curse for us; for it is written cursed is everyone that hangeth on a tree." Gal 3:13

The curses for breaking the law are listed in Deuteronomy 28 and they are poverty related.

STINGY SPIRIT
A stingy spirit is the manifestation of the spirit of poverty. The fear to give what you have to others, Jesus gave an example of a man who acquired so much and based his security on what he had but when death came nothing he had no answer. Jesus was teaching that a man's life does not consist in the material things we have.

The rich fool as the Bible describes got all he could and put his faith in the material. He was not interested in the need of others but was secured in the stuff he had gathered. God promised to bless Abraham and make him a blessing. The Bible records that Abraham and Sarah often entertained guests even angels, unawares.

Abraham was ready to give Isaac because he believed God could raise him back. God's purpose is to (a) bless, and (b) make you a blessing.

When the believer sees God as his source the economy does not change his desire to be a blessing. God as the source guarantees that the believer cannot run dry. When we obey God through tithes and given free will offerings we put ourselves in the position for God to bless us back.

Believers who do not give are living with fear of lack, some do not believe that if they give God the tithe which is a tenth of their income God is able to bless the ninety percent and make them experience sufficiency in their finances. It is a manifestation of the spirit of poverty. Yet the same people may live in good houses and drive nice cars.

On the other hand, I know people who do not have high income yet they give tithe faithfully because they love God and they believe God will take care of them. One earns much and gives little while the other earns little and gives much, who is freer?

A stingy spirit is a selfish spirit, this runs contrary to the spirit manifested by God the father who gave his only son freely to us. A person with a stingy spirit is bound to himself.

God had blessed Abraham, he was able to help Abraham to produce a son when he and his wife had waited for many years with no son in sight, Abraham tried to manufacture his own miracle when with the persuasion of his wife Sarah he fathers a son through their maid Hagar, and this brought contention at home.

God appears to him in Genesis 17 to remind him his plan was through his wife Sarah, Abraham quickly reminded God that not only was Sarah barren and past menopause his own body was also dead and impotent so a miracle was not possible.

He pleaded for Ishmael to be the channel of the blessing, God changes his name, he conforms to divine purpose circumcises himself and within a year Isaac was born. (Romans 4:17-21).

When God speaks to Abraham to put his son on the altar, Isaac represented his biggest blessing but he recognized without the help of God he and Sarah could not have had a baby since God is the source of Isaac he had no problem giving him back. In giving away his blessing, he realized a bigger purpose, God also offers his own son on the ranges of Mount Moriah where mount Calvary is situated.

Abraham had no fear of the future because God was his source; he was truly prosperous because his heart was in God not the blessing. He even believed if Isaac was sacrificed God could raise him up but God had prepared his own sacrifice.

END IN ITSELF
But seek ye first the kingdom of god, and his righteousness; and all these things shall be added unto you. **MATTHEW 6:33**

Beloved, I wish above all things that thou mayest proper and be in health, even as thy soul prospereth. **3 JOHN2**

A faithful man shall abound with blessings: but he that maketh haste to be rich shall not be innocent. **Proverbs 28:20**

But they that will be rich fall into temptation and a snare, and into many foolish and hurtful lusts, which drown men in destruction and perdition. **1TiMOTHY 6:9**

It is wrong to set as the primary goal in life making money or becoming wealthy. It has been taught that believers should succeed at all cost. On the contrary Jesus taught that we should seek the kingdom of God and all the material and financial blessings shall be added.

What does it mean to seek the kingdom of God, a kingdom is the domain of a king, a place where he reigns and his subjects are in submission to him, the king rules and has a way of doing things that differentiates his kingdom from others.

When we come to Jesus the kingdom of God comes to live within us, Jesus in the person of the Holy Spirit is Lord in our hearts. Though we live here we belong to another kingdom.

Our responsibility is to seek to the please the king, find out how things are done in the kingdom. One of the primary purposes of prosperity is establish the kingdom of God on the earth. Deuteronomy 8:18.

The reason for the believer's prosperity is not to make a name for himself or build a financial empire but to advance the kingdom of God. Yes, it is important for the believer to be blessed in order to be a blessing, when your blessings have no mission for the kingdom of God and ministry to humanity, it has failed to reach God's goal and is no different from any other rich unbeliever.

Many forget to invest in the kingdom through tithing, offerings, giving to the poor, orphans, supporting ministries, and outreaches and touching the lives of ordinary people around them. Our love for God and his kingdom should be paramount as we obey him in our giving.

Giving should not be seen as short cut to quick wealth, God wants our hearts and there is nothing we give that he did not first give us. Giving naturally opens the channel to receive because it is a law.

The following comments in the book *'Midas Touch'* by Kenneth Hagin is illuminating (pages 89-91)

> Our motive and purpose for giving should be pure and unselfish. We should do it because we love God. Giving is a natural expression of love. John 3:16 says, "God so loved the world that He gave." And we should do the same; we should give to God because we love Him.
>
> We should give to God in obedience to His Word. The Bible teaches us to give to the Lord and support His work. In addition to the scriptures we've already examined, there are many others that are unmistakable in their instruction about giving.

We should give as a means to help carry out Christ's Great Commission and support the work of those who are going into all the world with the Gospel.

We should give because we want to see people blessed. Our tithes and gifts help support outreaches of the local church and other organizations that minister to the poor, evangelize the lost and unreached, and build up the saints while equipping them for Christian service.

And, finally, way down the line, we should give in expectancy, believing God to honor the promises in His Word to bless and prosper us. Notice that I have listed five reasons to give, and I believe the order of this list reflects priorities that are very important. It seems to me that many preachers are overemphasizing number five and presenting that as the major reason for people to give.

Nevertheless, giving is a tried and proven way to plant seeds for a harvest that will result in our needs being met. The law of sowing and reaping does apply in the area of personal finances. The Bible is true when it says, "Give, and it shall be given unto you; good measure, pressed down, and shaken together, and running over, shall men give into your bosom. . ." (Luke 6:38).All of these are good and valid reasons for giving. And I believe they will lead to true prosperity — spirit, soul, and body.

When our motives for giving is pure God moves in our behalf, the believer is not giving to bribe God into blessing him, when you came to Jesus the blessing of Abraham came upon you. Galatians 3:13, it was the blessing of Abraham on the life of Joseph that caused him to have great favor although he found himself in a strange land, sold as a slave without family and friends to help him. The Bible says God blessed the house of Potiphar for Joseph's case. (Genesis 39:5)

In prison God was with him, he kept rising although from the natural standpoint he looked like a looser. It was the blessing that caused

Jacob to prosper after he had made mistakes, he ran away from home with a stick came back a prosperous man, it was the blessing that caused Isaac to sow in famine, in a strange land amidst a hostile people and he prospered. It was the covenant of blessing that worked in Daniel's life, he excelled in exile and was promoted above his fellows. It was this blessing that caused Abraham to leave home into a strange country where he found favor.

The covenant of blessing is operating in the believer's life today because Jesus a descendant of Abraham became a curse for us and all believers in him have received every blessing in the divine economy of Christ. Parents transfer their blood line, features, DNA to their children. If you belong to Jesus you are not under the curse of poverty you may not have loads of money and your pocket may have a gaping hole but you are redeemed from poverty.

In our ministry, we have been blessed to run an Orphanage, a community Maternity and Clinic, A Women and Youth Empowerment Centre, Primary and secondary Schools for Orphans. I remember when these projects began the question many asked me is what do we stand to gain from this? The education of the orphans, feeding and welfare as well as the Women and Youth Empowerment Centre programs are totally free. I was asked by many people that this is a third world country and it was unwise to make that kind of investment in people although we spend a lot the joy of giving is far greater.

Abraham was blessed but to become a blessing he was willing to sacrifice his blessing. Isaac was the promised child, God requested for him on Moriah he could have walked away from this in disobedience, as he raised the knife to slay his son God stopped him because he already prepared for himself a sacrifice.

But in that obedience Abraham's action released a greater blessing because on the ranges of Moriah is Mount Calvary where the Lord Jesus was crucified. Every tongue, people are race are coming to God because Abraham was truly a friend of God who held nothing back, He has become a blessing through the sacrifice of Christ to the whole world but his willingness to release Isaac was part of the process that released this blessing.

Believers must set their heart on God and not on things, making money at all cost is unscriptural. The word of God warns that those who must be rich at all cost will be shipwrecked.

But they that will be rich fall into temptation and a snare, and into many foolish and hurtful lusts, which drown men in destruction and perdition. **1TiMOTHY 6:9**

I have noticed people who set unrealistic standard in the name of prosperity. They can't wait for God to manifest his promises and usually result to gimmicks and tricks because it is not about seeking the kingdom but about their personal ambitions.

They can't give their desires to God because their desires are not submitted to the king. It is not about the kingdom of God it is about them. God promises that his blessings will overtake us as we seek his kingdom (Matt. 6:33).

It is God that brings the blessings, not man. When getting the blessings becomes an end, you are in trouble because you are already a blessed man if you are in Christ. When and how soon things materialize do not change the truth that you are blessed.. You are the blessed, you are the healed, and you are the righteous. Satan is only trying to steal your heritage,

GIMMICKS

"But have renounced the hidden things of dishonesty, not walking in craftiness, nor handling the word of God deceitfully but by manifestation of the truth commending ourselves to every man's conscience in the sight of God". **2CORINTHIANS 4:2**

"And the king of Sodom said unto Abram, Give me the persons, and take the goods to thyself. And Abram said to the king of Sodom, I have lift up mine hand unto the LORD, the most high God, the possessor of heaven and earth, That I will not take from a thread even to a shoelatchet, and that I will not take any thing that is thine, lest thou shouldest say I have made Abram rich Save only that which the young men have eaten and the portion of the

men which went with me, Aner, Eshcol, and Mamre; let them take their portion". **GENESIS 14:21-24**

"And Abram said unto Lot, Let there be no strife, I pray thee, between me and thee, and between my herdmen and thy herdmen for we be brethren. Is not the whole land before thee? separate thyself I pray thee, from me: if thou wilt take the left hand, then I will go to the right or if thou depart to the right hand, then I will go to the left. And Lot lifted up his eyes, and beheld all the plain of Jordan, that it was well watered everywhere, before the LORD destroyed Sodom and Gomorrah, even as the garden of the LORD, like the land of Egypt, as thou comest unto Zoar. Then Lot chose him all the plain of Jordan; and Lot journeyed east: and they separated themselves the one from the other.
Abram dwelled in the land of Canaan, and Lot dwelled in the cities of the plain, and pitched his tent toward Sodom. But the men of Sodom were wicked and sinners before the LORD exceedingly. And the LORD said unto Abram, after that Lot was separated from him, Lift up now thine eyes, and look from the place where

thou art northward, and southward, and eastward, and westward: For all the land which thou seest to thee will I give it and to thy seed forever. **GENESIS 13: 8-15**

Abraham had the chance to accumulate more after the battle with the kings but he refused to take that which might have been lawful he wanted it to be clear that God was the one blessing him and not man.

Abraham was not ready to struggle with Lot when there was strife he allowed him to take the good-looking land although it was on his account that Lot got any prosperity. The integrity and character of Abraham shines through, he wanted no short cuts if it was not God thing he did not want it, he was not out to get forward through any means that was at the least suspicious. Joseph refused to take a short cut to prosperity by refusing the advances of Potiphar's house.

Deceitful means of advancing such as fraud, cheating and gimmicks to raise money is a spirit of poverty in manifestation. This lack of integrity only shows that such blessings are not God given but a process of manipulation.

It is possible to meet your immediate needs, if God orders something he pays for it, it is difficult to sustain anything God has not started.

The person doing manipulation will have to invent new things to sustain the ministry, and becomes consumed by gimmicks.

A truly prosperous man can laugh at the face of the biggest needs; because he knows he is redeemed from the power of those forces that are responsible for that negative situation. What threat is a Zebra to a lion?

Pressure brings the best and worst out of people, a prosperous mind is a renewed mind, a mind that has been weaned from impatience, manipulation and carnality. Life is about choices when there are financial challenge believers and ministers must learn that a need can be met without God's approval, every kingdom has her own characteristic. The character of a kingdom emanates from the king, if we get things done contrary to the nature and character of the king our exercise is in futility.

Whatever we get must glorify the king, not we ourselves any answers that bring shame to the king are not a kingdom solution. The aroma of heaven must be on our blessing. Hollywood tactics, underhandedness have no place in the life of the believer.

Ministers may fall into the pitfall of unscrupulous tactics to raise money this has often made the church a laughing stock to the world. Gordon Lindsay's makes this comments in his book *Charismatic Ministry,* he wrote the following:

> [Money] is an important element in promoting Christian work. Its availability to a considerable extent governs the scope of our activities. It is, therefore, natural that a minister looks for ways and means by which he can secure necessary funds for the work that he feels called to do.
>
> But here lurks many pitfalls in which die unwary may stumble. The line between the permissible and the objectionable is sometimes very thin. Some men have raised hundreds of thousands of dollars

for missions, and their work is to be highly praised. Others have raised comparatively insignificant amounts, and the manner in which it was done or the way they used it, has called forth strong condemnation.

If people are told that the money is to be used for a certain purpose, and it is spent largely for other things, such as for promotion, then it is being raised under false pretenses. This is a sore point. Certainly there are costs in raising missionary money. Anyone who says otherwise doesn't speak the truth. But if the greater proportion of the funds so raised are used for overhead, then something is wrong...

The manner of taking offerings in a campaign is extremely important. If every service or a considerable number of services is occupied with a lengthy appeal for large offerings, the effect upon the people of the community is likely to be unfavorable. The ministers so engaged will soon be regarded as employed mainly in money raising. Gimmicks which included relics, bones, holy water, indulgences, etc., cursed the Medieval Church. They were widely used at that time as money-raising devices designed to appeal to people's ignorance and, superstition. Today certain preachers are resorting to gimmicks to entice people to part with their money. . . .

What we are referring to as gimmicks is the use of articles that purport to have some mysterious power or supposed virtue in them — a sort of charm or fetish — the use of which has no Scriptural foundation…
What are some of these gimmicks? The number apparently is endless, for new ones are heard of frequently.

The partial list includes such things as follows: a "blessed purse" that causes money to multiply "supernaturally"; the "gift" of prosperity; "magic pictures" in which the image reappears after the person has closed his eyes...; a special "prayer carpet"; "holy oil" or "holy water" that is supposed to carry a special virtue; cloths which "supernaturally" change color; "blessed nails"; "blessed pictures"; "blessed sawdust" on which an angel is supposed to have walked; a barrel of water in which an angel comes down and "troubles it";

"bottled demons," etc. These are only a few of the long list of gimmicks which have been offered to the public.

The Reformation actually had its beginning when Martin Luther became convinced that all the gimmicks the church used — the relics, the saints' bones, splinters from the "true cross," etc. — were phony and had no virtue. May God help the minister to abide in the simplicity and purity of the gospel and not attempt to mislead people with things.

COVETOUSNESS

We need to draw line is thin between seeking the kingdom of God and his righteousness and having all things added and seeking things and having the kingdom added. I liken it to a wheel with the knob in the centre; every spoke rotates around the knob. In seeking the kingdom we must keep the focus on the Lord, who is the centre of the knob and allow other thing in our lives to rotate around him.

Sometimes when people come in contact with the message of prosperity one or two things happen. Some feel "thank God I can change my destiny by obeying God's laws in this area", for others the spirit of greed and covetousness take over.

COVETOUSNESS IS LUST FOR THE THINGS OF OTHERS, A PASSION TO ACCUMULATE THINGS AS BASIS FOR SECURITY.
Poverty thinking makes people feel that their life is measured by what they posses which is opposite of what Jesus said.

This does not mean you should not live well but by basing your worth and status in life on how many cars, houses and material things is vain, this means rich unbelievers have more value than believers who don't have the same material acquisition. Jesus however taught that if you had the whole world and was not saved it profits you nothing.

Jesus also said in Luke 12:15 *And he said unto them, Take heed and beware of covetousness: for a man's life consisteth not in the abundance of the things which he possesseth*

Once you set material things as the barometer to gauge who you are and determine your status and security you'd end up chasing things and you are not different from any unsaved person with such goals. You'll never be able to say like Paul I know how to be abased and abound. A man whose worth is based on the car he drives will lose his joy if something goes wrong with that car because his worth is being destroyed. When material things go up you go up, when they come down you come down.

It is sad that ignorant believers or those who have not been well taught relate to people strictly from the material, natural or financial stand point. When we use the material and the mundane to judge and value a believer then the work of Calvary is not valued as our basis for self-worth and security.

We invariably practice respect of persons. A minister reported attending a meeting where the criterion for allocating accommodation to attendees was done on the basis of the value of the cars they drove to the meeting.

It is carnal and pathetic. How do we value other believers? Is it on the basis of their material wellbeing or their spirituality?

Ye lust, and have not: ye kill and desire to have, and cannot obtain: ye fight and war, yet ye have not, because ye ask not. Ye ask, and receive not, because ye ask amiss, that ye may consume it upon your lusts. **JAMES 4:2-3**

Once material things become the yardstick for prosperity in your life you'd find that you are engaged in competition with others. If the other brother gets a new car you must get a new car or at least something new. "Godliness with contentment is great gain", (1 Timothy 6:19) There is nothing wrong with things but to watch Christians and ministers talk and live you can come away with the impression that we are only here for the mundane.

The impression created is misleading and shocking because what engages their attention is all in the natural, things and more things. We need to have our needs met but to live with an insatiable desire for more is bondage. A believer who loses his joy over the latest thing he has not yet acquired is carnal and only living for the material realm and in that respect not different from the unsaved.

What message does that give to the unbeliever?

Covetousness stops the flow of divine prosperity. Being content is not settling down with poverty but not building your lives around things. Some believers get so miserable if they can't get that outfit or if some blessing is delayed. I can't picture Jesus becoming depressed because the suit he planned to preach in was not available.

I can't picture him having a fit because he walked to the meeting instead of riding a donkey, (of course, riding a donkey is better than walking because you are less exhausted). One minister arrived in a foreign country but refused to leave the airport because the car they brought to fetch him was below his dignity, sat for hours until another car was brought, that is a manifestation of insecurity and the spirit of poverty.

Once the devil knows that your life consists in things and your perceived value is based on material acquisition, he'll tighten the noose around your neck for he knows that once you don't have enough, materially, or that things are stalled, you'd be gripping and complaining.

He also knows that you'd be doing everything and any-thing to protect what you see as your real worth, either by fraudulent-means or simply by trying to acquire a larger image just to prove that you are still materially sufficient. I have observed people who cannot pay their basic bills going into debts to show their brothers in Christ that they are prosperous. It seems to me that that is a cloak of covetousness or plain foolishness.

And Abraham said to Lot, let there be no strife, I pray there, between me and thee, and between my herdmen and thy herdmen; for we be brethren. Is not the whole land before thee? Separate thyself, I pray thee, from me: If thou wilt take the left hand, then I will go to the right; or if thou depart to the right hand, then I will go to the left. **GENESIS 13: 8-9**

The blessing of the Lord, it maketh rich, and he addeth no sorrow with it. **PROVERBS 10:22**

The story of Abraham and Lot is a story that shows that a man who truly believes that God will prosper him needs not be a covetous.

Abraham was not worried that Lot wanted the good land because Abraham believed that God is faithful to take care of him. Abraham was not involved in manipulating the situation, he had enough seed in the ground, he was a tither and knew he had a covenant with God.

Ministries that promise people would be millionaires if they gave an amount in a fortnight are trying to play God. These actions are motivated by fear and lack of trust that God will provide for them. It is a spirit of poverty in demonstration and is driven by fear. it says get it at all cost. Blessing of God maketh rich and addeth no sorrow (Proverbs 10:22).

If God is the source we don't need to violate the Bible to help him. Christians who cheat on tax also manifest the spirit of poverty. God does not contradict himself.

CHEATING IS NOT GOD'S WAY FORWARD. Lot was enamored by the beauty of Sodom this became his undoing as the spirit of that city brought destruction to his family.

One would have expected Lot to give Abraham his uncle the right to choose first when the strife broke out but his covetousness and need to get forward prevented this. Abraham being a blessed man knew that although his land was taken the blessing was in him.

After Lot had departed God told Abraham that all the land including Lot's acquisition were his.

LOW PERCENTAGE GIVING

41 ¶ And Jesus sat over against the treasury, and beheld how the people cast money into the treasury: and many that were rich cast in much. {money: a piece of brass money} And there came a certain poor widow, and she threw in two mites, which make a farthing. {mites: it is the seventh part of one piece of that brass money}
And he called unto him his disciples, and saith unto them, Verily I say unto you, that this poor widow hath cast more in than all they which have cast into the treasury: For all they did cast in of their abundance but she of her want did

cast in all that she had even all her living. **Mark 12**

The widow's mite (Mk 12:41-42) was important because she did not manifest the spirit of poverty. She looked unto God a spirit of poverty would have kept that money back.

The percentage of her giving was hundred percent. Jesus said she gave more than all the people who gave bigger amounts. In the case of Elijah and the Widow of Zerephath, she gave her life and that of her son.

The focus a times is one the amount, some who put large amounts that have cost them nothing are given so much recognition when in actual fact God may see that as poor giving.

When some give large amounts, they want it known and is some cases run the application of the funds themselves, when God is our source and we are not inhibited by the spirit of poverty, we should give without calling every ones' attention and with simplicity. Those who give after much persuasion and personal representation are flesh driven and attention seeking.

There are churches that have to run around certain members every time there is a need, they may give a large amount which may not be there best but they enjoy that spirit of dependence. The Pastor who engages in this type of practice must also walk on needles and needles to keep such donors and their families happy. You don't need them if God is your source he will send people who will give their best and not turn you into a beggar.

NO NICE THINGS?

There came unto him a woman having an alabaster box of very precious ointment, and poured it on his head, as he sat at meat. But when his disciples saw it, they had indignation, saying, to what purpose is this waste? For this anointment might have been sold for much and given to the poor. When Jesus understood it, he said unto them, why trouble ye the woman? For she hath wrought a good work upon me. **MATTHEW 26:7-10**

Every good gift and every perfect gift is from above and cometh down from the father of lights, with whom is no variableness, neither shadow of turning. **JAMES 1:17**

The thief cometh not, but for to steal, and to kill, and to destroy: I am come that they might have life, and that they might have it more abundantly. **JOHN 10:10**

Ps 68:19 *Blessed be the Lord, who daily loadeth us with benefits, even the God of our salvation. Selah.*

Believers need not be apologetic about beautiful blessings that God loads them with. Believers sometimes hide their blessing to avoid persecution as though it is a crime to be blessed by God.

In Matt 26:7-10, Jesus was anointed with very expensive perfumes and some people around him his disciples felt this was a waste. There are blessings that will come into a faithful believer's life because of his obedience to the laws of God. I have had God blessed me with things that I would not have bought myself. God will give those things if he can trust you.

God did not create all the beautiful things on earth for devil and his crowd but for the enjoyment of his children and propagation of his kingdom. When the blessing overtakes you it humbles you because you are not driven by greed and competition. The religious idea is that God uses people and wants them to have nothing; I have noticed that the families of such people if they are ministers of the gospel often turn against them, because the children cannot understand that God forgot to give them a pay day despite the enormous sacrifices.

Some who hold this view secretly despise and covet the good things others have. God wants our hearts not to be in things but in him, he can then trust us with any level of blessing, without us defining our identity and status by those things. We can keep a grateful and humble attitude and love those who persecute us for the blessings of God. Persecution is part of the bargain.

This excerpts from the book Drawn by His Holiness shed more light

Drawn By His Love — The Life of Holiness Jerry Savelle

The same self-centered attitude that the world has, is being brought into the

Church. The only reason some people ever study the Bible, their only motivation for learning anything about faith, is just to try to get some of the "things" they are lusting after. If that is your motive for studying the Word of God, you should know it is not pleasing to Him.

God wants us in His Word so we can know Him. In fact, the very first reason for our having faith is not so we can have things, but so we can please God. So we can declare the praises of Him Who called us out of darkness into His wonderful light. And pleasing God has its rewards. Solomon tells us: When a man's ways please the Lord, he maketh even his enemies to be at peace with him (Prov. 16:7).

Don't Get Satisfied
I don't want to leave the impression that God does not want us to believe for / the things we need. He does. But when / that becomes our only motive, it is not pleasing to Him. I served as pastor of a church for six years. During that time I

counseled many people who had no idea what a relationship with God was all about. All they wanted was a formula to get things. Some kind of "get-rich-quick" scheme. There are no such things in the Bible. God doesn't have any formulas for us to run through our little computer to get rich overnight.

(I would suggest that if anyone offers you some kind of formula like that, you'd better check it out very carefully. It is probably illegal.) God doesn't have a formula, He has a lifestyle. He says that if you and I will adopt that lifestyle and live by it, eventually it will produce fruit — the fruit of righteous living.

Some people serve God only because of some good thing He might do for them. I wonder how many people would serve God today if He were to announce: "I want you to serve Me, but henceforth I am discontinuing all blessings." I'm afraid if God made such an announcement as that, the result would be like Gideon's army of ten thousand who were put to the test to cull out those who were afraid or unfit for duty.

(Judges 7:1-7.) God would look around and there would be about 300 left!

Why am I serving God? Because of His blessings? No. I am serving God because I love Him. I will serve Him all my days whether He ever does anything for me or not.

if God didn't do anything for us at all but cause us to escape an eternity in hell, that is reason enough to shout for glory! But the truth is, that's not all He can and will do for us – both in this life and in the life to come.

Yes, god has promised to make us the head and not the tail, above and not beneath, to bless us coming in and going out, to bless us in the city and in the field. Yes, God has promised to give us a surplus of property and abundant life. Yes, God has promised that we will reign with Him as kings and priests. All that is true. And marvelous.

But what God needs right now is a people who would serve Him even if they never had a one of those promises. A people who love Him so much they are determined to be obedient and faithful to Him if they never see a better car, or a better home, or more money. That's the kind of people God is looking for. God wants sincerity of heart.

CHAPTER 4

VISION

Where there is no vision, the people perish but he that keepeth the law, happy is he. **PROVERBS 29:18**

He made known his ways unto Moses, his acts unto the children of Israel. **PSALMS. 103:7**

Vision is defined as looking ahead, grasping the truth that underlines the fact, or an underlying truth.

A vision deals with purposes: why am I doing it this way? What is the reason or purpose of an action? What is the vision? If you don't have a vision for your business, when certain challenges come up you may not know what to do. Therefore, the ways of God is the underlying truth in a vision. When you set the course of your direction with the higher purposes of God, you are not easily sidetracked by everything that comes your way. Moses knew the purposes of God and was focused; when the children of Israel drifted he remained focused on the goal.

The vision you have or the purpose will help you in your decision making when you face the challenges of life. Challenging situations do not change your direction; you already know what to do because you have a vision or direction.

Joseph and Daniel had a vision and purpose for their lives therefore did not struggle to do right. Daniel was not ready to defile himself, Joseph did not want to sin against God.

God showed Moses not only where to go or what to do, but why he had to do so, to establish a people who would worship God. He showed Moses at the Burning bush that it was time for the covenant he had with Abraham to be fulfilled, to bring them into the land of promise and make them a model for other nations. For many in Israel their vision was food, water, shelter and comfort, anytime these were affected their devotion to God was challenged, they did not see the bigger picture.

Visions are cardinal; they hold a house together like foundations of a house on which you build. You cannot build contrary to the vision or design you have laid. The Bible says, "No other foundation can anyone lay other than that which has been laid which is Christ" (1 Cor. 3:11).When there were problems some of the children of Israel wanted to return to Egypt and jettison the vision, but that will be equivalent to removing the foundations of a house.

The church is built on the foundation laid by the Bible, Apostles and prophets. God cannot give you a revelation different from the Holy book. You may discover some-thing that has been revealed already in the Bible but you cannot write we cannot write any books that have the same authority as the Bible. Today some have their own revelations which you can't find in the Bible.

The vision is the cornerstone that makes the building stand together. Why did the children of Israel have problems with Moses? It was because Moses understood the vision of God, they didn't. God was trying to make them a special people through whom he'd change the world, but they were only concerned about food and comfort.

That was the reason why anytime they did not see miracles they murmured and complained again and again. They were ready to return to Egypt and were ready to fashion other gods, this is a similar mindset to people who do not care how a miracle is received or how they come about their answers.

If there is a delay they try something else, once it sounds, looks and feels like the Holy Ghost they are all for it. This is deception. Many in Israel died because of God's judgment when they were worshipped other gods, they rebelled against God and lusted after things he planned for them to have. Israel did not know how to handle delays when there were no quick answers, they complained and compromise. They failed in comprehending the plans of God for their future, they wanted immediate answers, and they wanted to be like the nations around them.

The children of Israel knew what God was doing but not why. God gave the children of Israel gold before they left Egypt as compensation for all the misery, but he had a higher purpose in mind, he wanted those precious things to be used in the building of the tabernacle, Israel missed the point they turned the gold into a golden calf which they worshipped. The goal of prosperity is to bless us and to also establish God's kingdom, when we fail to grasp that our blessings become an idol.

Some people today understand what of prosperity and not the why? Children may understand what they need but not why. If your three-year-old son asked you for a double barrel gun will you oblige him? Why not? He wants fun but may end up killing others and is a threat to himself. This is reason why God has not been able to commit much to believers.

In a marriage situation, if both couples don't have a vision for their home, they will go with the crowd and follow other people's visions for family life. If you don't have a vision for what you're doing you'll discover you're tossed to and fro by every wind of doctrine that blows around.

The things God has revealed by His word cannot be changed, they are eternally established. They are foundations and pillars of truth. There must be a vision, the underlining truth governing your life. The more the believer grasps the vision, the more effective he will become.

It is important to communicate vision to co-laborers; the why of the vision, then you'll experience better performance on the job. The tower of Babel reached the height it did because the people were building with one mind and one vision and the Bible records that nothing would have been withheld from them.

Those who built the tower of Babel although their purpose was not agreeable to God's will committed themselves to something bigger they made sacrifice for their goals.

Can two walk together except they be agreed?
AMOS 3:3

There should be unity in the things done in the local church or ministry even though we're fulfilling different parts of the same vision. An orchestra is enjoyed based on the symphony they make, and not in the discordant notes.

Nobody pays to listen to discordant tunes. Whoever you are following, make sure he has a vision; you can't follow a car that is parked but one which is moving. If a blind man leads another, they'll both fall in the ditch (Matt. 15:14).

When there is no vision people change directions constantly, one day they are headed north, the next day if they hear of some successful person going south they turn around and head south, they waver and no one knows where they are going to next. Jesus is the head of the church.

When he ascended into heaven he gave gifts unto the church, apostles, prophets, teachers, evangelists (Eph. 4:12). Whatever visions we have in the ministry are his own, not ours. God calls a man he gives a vision and he calls others to be part of that vision. John.6:44 says *'No man can come to me except the father draws him* In every church and ministry there is always a church within the church, they're the people that identity with what the ministry is doing and want to be part of it. They're the real church in the church.

You cannot accomplish a vision all by yourself if God does not bring people who identify with it. If a man tries to run his home alone he'll soon find out he needs his wife. Agreement is spirit, soul, and body, in the way you think and in the way you act. If your actions do not show that you're in agreement with the ministry then you're not in agreement.

There must be synchronizing of spirit, soul and body, so also all arms of a ministry must synchronize. It is not everyone doing the same thing or working in the same office but having the same purpose. Had the Israelites all known why God led them the problems would have been less.

VISION MUST BE UNDERSTOOD
"And the Lord answered me and said, write the vision, and make it plain upon tables, that he may run that readeth it". **HABAKKUK2:2**

If the vision is not plain or understood, you cannot run with it. What you don't understand, you're against. If you take time to explain the vision, you'll have agreement from others.

Leaders need to effectively communicate instructions down to the others. Where a worker does not understand the vision of any department he needs to ask the person who's above him instead of doing his own thing.

The vision needs to be plain; easy to understand so that anyone who comes in to serve can understand where they are headed. The vision should not be a mystery, if it is a mystery only the person with the vision can achieve it. If a leader is leading and no one is following he is walking alone.

There will always be aspects of the ministry that God will communicate to you directly as the set person, the one with the mandate or commission for the work. A leader is not a dictator he needs to show the way, some believe that there should be no clear leader and everyone should be equal. It is a recipe for chaos and disorder because anything with more than one head is a monster.

In Exodus 24:1, it was Moses God called up, and not Aaron; Moses took seventy elders with him, God knows the chain of command and does not run a democracy.

There is something you can tap from a man that God has placed in authority and influence if you humble yourself, something of him can rub off on you. It might be the gifts of the spirit or a special anointing.

Anointing comes by association environment and influence; visions could be strengthened the same way. For example, if you want God to use you in the area of healing, you cannot despise those used in the area of healing.

A critical attitude will harm your ministry. With a critical attitude, you can go through a ministry but the ministry will not go through you. Your attitude towards leadership will affect what rubs off on you. SOME PEOPLE UNDER GOOD LEADERSHIP IMPROVE, OTHERS DEPRECIATE - ALL DEPENDS ON THEIR ATTITUDE.

God's packaging program is not always what we'll call ideal. Why on earth would God choose stammering Moses when Aaron and

Miriam were there? God chose Samson, Peter, Jacob, Saul, David, Solomon and all the others despite the weaknesses in their characters which he knew about. God does not need the benefit of hindsight he already knows the future from the beginning. God chooses the weak things of the world to confound the wise.

The person God puts over you may not be rich or educated or as old as you are. If you despise and disrespect them you cannot be a partaker of the grace upon them. The Bible teaches us clearly that, the powers that be are ordained of-God.

Jesus took twelve disciples initially and later seventy because if he multiplied himself in seventy people more of the work could be done. God does not work by quota system; he works with the available and faithful ones.

But unfortunately, some in the body are not concerned about excellence and quality. In a military sense it takes more time to prepare those in the special regiments they may be fewer in number than the general troop but highly effective.

God wants to see quality in the work we do, a large congregation does not translate into a strong army.

Jesus tried to communicate his vision to his disciples, as much as he felt they could handle at a time. Where he started with them was not where they ended. A leader should locate his people and move them gradually with his vision. God does the same so people don't faint. Too much too soon can great panic and apathy.

CHAPTER 5

LEADERSHIP

SELF PRESERVATION

"And the Philistines gathered themselves together to fight with Israel, thirty thousand chariots, and six thousand horsemen, and people as the sand which is on the sea shore in multitude: and they came up and pitched in Michmash, eastward from Bethaven.

When the men of Israel saw that they were in a strait (for the people were distressed then the people did hide themselves in caves, and in thickets, and in rocks, and in high places, and in pits. And some of the Hebrews went over Jordan to the land of Gad and Gilead. As for

Saul, he was yet in Gilgal, and all the people followed him trembling.

And he tarried seven days, according to the set time that Samuel had appointed: but Samuel came not to Gilgal; and the people were scattered from him. And Saul said Bring hither a burnt offering to me, and peace offerings. And he offered the burnt offering. And it came to pass, that as soon as he had made an end of offering the burnt offering, behold, Samuel came and Saul went out to meet him, that he might salute him.

And Samuel said What hast thou done And Saul said Because I saw that the people were scattered from me, and that thou camest not within the days appointed, and that the Philistines gathered themselves together at Michmash; Therefore said I, The Philistines will come down now upon me to Gilgal, and I have not made supplication unto the LORD: I forced myself therefore, and offered a burnt offering.

And Samuel said to Saul, Thou hast done foolishly thou hast not kept the commandment of the LORD thy God, which he commanded thee: for now would the LORD have established thy kingdom upon Israel forever. **1 Samuel 13:5-13**

Saul had a vision to preserve his throne but had little concern about the presence of God or his approval. It was not a problem for him to disobey the Lord in order to please people.

When the people began to go away because Prophet Samuel delayed his arrival he forced himself to make a sacrifice thus intruding into the wrong office. He was ready to do anything to preserve his throne but not ready to pay the price of God's presence, he paid dearly.

When a leader needs to succeed at all cost there is no telling how far such a person would go in this instance Saul intruded into another office which he was not called into. All that mattered to Saul was to stay in power, although the position he occupied came by divine choice not manipulation. The cheers of the people must not deaden the voice of God, Saul's desperation was so severe that towards the end of his life he requests the help of a witch to solve God's problem. It has been quoted by some that what is important is bring people to Jesus this is risky.

Some have been known to sear their consciences in times of great desperation by consulting cultic people for help. The shame of all this is that these cultic people boast about the visits of such people and how they assisted them to solve their problems.

When the lines of righteousness, decorum, bible-based Christianity are eroded, the emerging syncretism makes it easier for a backslidden minister to justify visits to such places with the excuse that they use the name of Jesus also.

The king of Israel was in the house of a witch, who he was supposed to destroy, he wanted to keep the kingdom at all cost no wonder Jesus said that which is esteemed amongst men is an abomination before God.

Leadership is not about self-preservation and empire building; an insecure leader sees every emerging leader as a threat, any other ministry advancement is viewed as competition. This precisely was the problem when David killed

Goliath and the women sang his praises and Saul became insanely jealous that he tried to kill the young man.

When ministries and churches compete to the point where they out price each other for places to rent for worship, you have to ask whose kingdom and in whose name. If God has placed you somewhere he will keep there, every one's calling is unique, when God set out the assignment he also created people who can fulfill it, and you are tailor made for your ministry.

Your birth, parentage, experience, qualifications are all orchestrated by God so you can fit into that assignment, there is no point going somewhere you were not made to be, carrying out an assignment you were not designed to be.

A crop that is planted in its natural environment will flourish, uproot the same crop to another environment and it will wither, the problem is not with the crop it is with the location. Don't try to live out another's destiny, don't be enamored with the attraction of Sodom, when Lot was uprooted from his place through strife he ended up in Sodom and Sodom ended his ministry.

Eccl 10:4 ¶ *If the spirit of the ruler rise up against thee, leave not thy place; for yielding pacifieth great offences.*

Leaving your place because of offence can lead to displacement. It is important how he leave a place because this often affects how we enter into a new place. It is good to deal with offences, bless people, ensure that we have nothing n our hearts against others and leave with a blessing. Without clear direction, a man driven by offence may end up at a wrong location as he is seeking rest, when the emotions are troubled he may have problems hearing God clearly.

"And Samuel said When thou wast little in thine own sight, wast thou not made the head of the tribes of Israel, and the LORD anointed thee king over Israel? And the LORD sent thee on a journey, and said Go and utterly destroy the sinners the Amalekites, and fight against them until they be consumed {they...: Heb. they consume them}

Wherefore then didst thou not obey the voice of the LORD, but didst fly upon the spoil, and didst evil in the sight of the LORD? And Saul said unto Samuel, Yea, I have obeyed the voice of the LORD, and have gone the way which the LORD sent me, and have brought Agag the king of Amalek, and have utterly destroyed the Amalekites.

But the people took of the spoil, sheep and oxen, the chief of the things which should have been utterly destroyed, to sacrifice unto the LORD thy God in Gilgal. And Samuel said Hath the LORD as great delight in burnt offerings and sacrifices, as in obeying the voice of the LORD? Behold, to obey is better than sacrifice, and to hearken than the fat of rams. For rebellion is as the sin of witchcraft, and stubbornness is as iniquity and idolatry. Because thou hast rejected the word of the LORD, he hath also rejected thee from being king". {witchcraft: Heb. divination}. **1 Samuel 15:17-23**

God told Saul to destroy everything. Saul lied to Samuel that he had obeyed the voice of the Lord.

The opposite of obedience is stubbornness which is as idolatry. Saul ought to have done what the Lord told him to do, but he didn't and God took away his kingdom from him because of disobedience.

A servant cannot run his own plans, Saul connived with the people and spared the king and the best of the spoil, and he obeyed God partially which is disobedience. Whatever we compromise to get will ultimately be lost, God is no respecter of persons, and the voice of the people is not necessarily the voice of God. Saul's goal was to stay connected with the people to assure his throne.

When God gives an instruction, it is good to follow it to the letter. Saul's rebellion didn't start in one day. He offered sacrifice he was not supposed to offer, his heart was hardening and he had no problem with sparing the best flock and the king.

When we hear of heinous things done by others, we must never think about ourselves too highly and feel we cannot make a slip because any one who indulges his flesh will fall. A gradual slow slide is less noticeable than a big thud.

You may well be rebelling quietly even as church- goers. For example, you're not a pastor and you decide to usurp that function, you may do it but it won't be like the man that was anointed for it. When you find out your anointing is disappearing from you, ask yourself if you're functioning within the call.

If a prophet decides to become an evangelist, he might lose the anointing of a prophet.. Saul had been backsliding a long time; Saul lost the kingdom to a younger man because he would not obey simple instructions. He broke his ranks and God was angry with him.

BE A JESUS DONKEY

There are lots of lessons we can learn from the donkey Jesus rode into Jerusalem. In this donkey, we find a good example of how a true servant of God needs to be. In using this donkey as a metaphor for leadership we can glean many precious truths.

"And when they came nigh to Jerusalem, unto Bethphage and Bethany, at the mount of

Olives, he sendeth forth two of his disciples, And saith unto them, Go your way into the village over against you: and as soon as ye be entered into it, ye shall find a colt tied whereon never man sat loose him, and bring him.

And if any man say unto you, Why do ye this? say ye that the Lord hath need of him; and straightway he will send him hither.

And they went their way and found the colt tied by the door without in a place where two ways met; and they loose him.

And certain of them that stood there said unto them, What do ye loosing the colt? And they said unto them even as Jesus had commanded and they let them go. And they brought the colt to Jesus, and cast their garments on him; and he sat upon him.

And many spread their garments in the way: and others cut down branches off the trees, and strawed them in the way. And they that went before and they that followed cried saying Hosanna; Blessed is he that cometh in the name of the Lord: Blessed be the kingdom of our father David, that cometh in the name of the Lord: Hosanna in the highest. **Mark 11:1-10**

CALL AND TRAINING

"Before I formed thee in the belly I knew thee; and before thou camest forth out of the womb I sanctified thee, and I ordained thee a prophet unto the nations". **Jeremiah 1:5**

"For ye see your calling, brethren, how that not many wise men after the flesh, not many mighty, not many noble, are called: But God hath chosen the foolish things of the world to confound the wise; and God hath chosen the weak things of the world to confound the things which are mighty; And base things of the world, and things which are despised hath God chosen yea, and things which are not, to bring to nought things that are. That no flesh should glory in his presence. **1 Corinthians 1:26-29**

The colt Jesus requested was tied up, no one had ever ridden on it, and no one seemed to know his purpose. Destinies are tied before the Lord calls us and breaks us before we walk into his purpose.

The same is true of every man, God created us for his glory and until we come to Jesus we are barely existing, instead of remarking about what we gave up to serve the Lord we ought to be grateful that he found us and released us into our destinies. It is incredible that Jesus would take a donkey which had not been ridden and get on it straight away, in the natural this is not possible the donkey needed to be broken but Jesus been the creator could do this. A believer who is used of God also needs to be broken so he does not pose a threat to himself and others and after being used he becomes a cast away.

Jesus himself is our example in the training and the dealings of God for the maturation of our true destinies.

The stages of growth for a child of God are very similar to natural growth. When a baby is born the whole family rejoices, much so when the baby is healthy, similarly there is joy in heaven over one sinner that comes to repentance because another carbon copy of Christ is born in the spirit with the spiritual capacity to be like God. Jesus is the first begotten from the dead and the others rose from death to live and look like him.

When Jesus first came into the earth, born of the spirit he was a baby in a manger but he was not ready to take on the world and save man from sin. Perhaps one of the most notable differences between Jesus the second and the first Adam was that Adam was created full grown and had no opportunity to grow.

It is important to note that Jesus grew and was trained he went from babyhood to childhood in the manger when the shepherds came he was a baby, when the wise men came he was a child in the house, at age twelve he had matured enough to speak with the scholars and the elders of the day in the temple.

After this memorable outing at the temple, he went back home to his parents and was subject to them, he carried on as a carpenter with his father and did whatever was necessary for his training.

In Hebrews 5:7-9 Jesus learnt obedience.
"Who in the days of his flesh, when he had offered up prayers and supplications with strong crying and tears unto him that was able to save him from death, and was heard in that he feared; Though he were a Son, yet learned he obedience by the things which he suffered;

And being made perfect, he became the author of eternal salvation unto all them that obey him;

EVERY SON MUST BE TRAINED
Jesus said he had come to serve and give his life as ransom for many; it took him some thirty years to be ready to fulfill this mission. Had he not gone through all the training his commission required he would have reneged on his assignment in the garden of Gethsemane.

In today's world Jesus would have had to answer questions about his paternity, many who knew his modest background questioned his authority for doing all the miracles he per formed. Some wondered how a carpenter's son could boast of great power.

At his home town there was community unbelief and ridicule and he had to leave and could not bless them. As a result of his birth many had lost their own children through the massacre that took place when Herod tried to kill Jesus, Jesus definitely caused eye brows to be raised by families who lost their children because of him. He took it well because his acceptance was not based on the opinion of men.

Jesus learnt to put his flesh under and submit to the will of God where his appetites were concerned, when Satan tempted him he offered food knowing he had been without food a long while, Jesus had mastered his appetites and passion he had learnt to put his body under.

This is an important test to pass because the flesh has caused many a servant of God to fall. Food, pleasure, pornography, adultery, fornication, anger, malice, jealousy and other works of the flesh are potential pit falls that sons of God who want to serve him must learn to deal with.

 The devil showed him all the glory, the riches, wealth and splendor of the world. Jesus was not looking for any blessing from the devil; he had left treasures in heaven to come here and won't be deterred from his mission. Gold and silver are part of the tools for ministry but must not become a god. The goal of a minister must not be to gather riches; his goal must be to allow wealth to serve him.

There is a fine line between materialism and prosperity. The primary goal of God's blessing is to bless his children so they would in turn establish the kingdom, unlike the rich young ruler in the Bible who gathered all his riches into barns, afraid of the rainy day, his trust was in money, he was not a giver and did not see beyond himself.

His motto seemed to be "get all you can and can all you get". He lived for himself and money was his God. God's servant must not fall into the trap of arranging meetings for the sake of gathering money. God has prepared enough resources for all his assignments.

PASSING THE TESTS OF LEADERSHIP
The eagle is the Christian ideally considered, the eagle goes through a process of training to prepare it for life outside the nest. She is moved out of the comfort of the nest and is repeatedly allowed to fall from great heights when she thinks she is not going to make it the mother eagle comes to her rescue, after this process is repeated severally, it dawns on the eagle that she's got a pair of wings like her mother and begins to use them.

God allows challenging situations our way to help us develop character; a test may be repeated severally in our lives until we produce the required fruit, which is to our advantage and survival.

I remember many years ago my wife and I were invited to minister in another country, after paying our way we soon discovered that our host was in financial crisis and we had to take care of him and ourselves during the mission.

It turned out that there was no honorarium, we had not only paid our way but had also looked after the family of our host meeting their financial needs. My flesh wanted to protest but the Lord said we were to do this as a service to him, as we got on the plane back home I heard his voice, he said 'you have passed another test'. In a matter of months tremendous doors were opened in that country for us and the provision was enormous. In real life, a donkey also goes through a process before it can be used for different purposes, God trains his servants so they will be ready for their assignments. The Lord Jesus was tempted at every point yet without sin, he was ready.

When Isaac was weaned Abraham celebrated, Samuel went to Shiloh after he was weaned tests will not end but preparation is as important as the actual ministry because in real combat they do not use blank bullets, you can get killed as well as get others killed. The late Lester Sumrall in his book *'Pioneers of Faith'* had some advice for younger ministers as he warns against pitfalls of ministry. These are avoidable as we allow the Lord to prepare and protect us.

Spiritual Revolution Is on the Way

Now, I believe the greatest spiritual revolution in the history of the world is about to take place. I am not sure all Christians will be in on it, because it might be too "radical." It may be too "off-beat." Preachers may not look dignified. The gifts of the Spirit will function mightily, moving governments and frightening political leaders. God's Church will come alive just before Jesus comes.

There will be some mainline denominational people who cannot bridge the gap any more than they did in the past. There will be some Pentecostals and Charismatic who cannot bridge the gap. There will be some Word of Faith leaders who cannot bridge the gap. People will say, "That's too far for me to jump from where I am. I'm going to stick it out right here. I'm comfortable where I am."

That is the reason people in other moves of God did not go with the flow of the Holy Spirit. They stayed where they were comfortable. I have asked God many times, "Please do not do anything while I am alive unless you let me be a part of it."

I promise you, when a new thrust of the Spirit comes, I will not criticize it. I will not find fault with it. I will just receive it and accept it. For those in it who need help, I will try to teach them to get on the right track to be what God wants them to be. Someone needs to be there to hold it together, to love the people, to forgive the little things that are not right.

I believe we are on the verge of a spontaneous move of God. No one has a corner on the blessings of God. The only one who can eliminate you from the blessings of God is yourself. Many of you reading this book will be here when Jesus comes, so you will want to be in the last blaze of glory!

Do not expect your denomination or even your church to come with you, but do not curse them if they will not. Do not judge them and call them names. Just move with God yourself.

No organized group ever moved into a new revelation — only individuals do. Organizations come later, when enough individuals have received the new move. Be a person who moves with God wherever He wants you to be. Keep your heart open and say, "I will be a recipient of whatever you give, Lord."

In more than sixty years of ministry, I have never been sidelined with some stupid doctrine. I never budged in any direction. I believe and teach now what I did when I was a teenager — the same gospel, the same truth, the same anointing, the same power. I am not afraid of anything the devil does.

If something is not right, you can say, "You aren't right according to the Bible. Line yourself up with the Bible or keep your mouth shut."
Very simple! If you will stand that way, you will always abide in truth.

I have been constantly in God's blessing every day of my life. You cannot retire from a blessing. If you are a healing preacher, and you stop going to healing meetings for about ten years then think you're going to jump back in and do the same thing, forget it! You will be as a tinkling cymbal, an empty drum. If you want God's blessings, you have to follow Him constantly.

I have preached for some of the great pioneers when their properties were being taken away. I encouraged them,

"It does not matter about the property. God will give you another piece of property. Just stick with the blessings of God."

Jesus is coming soon. Let us fill the earth with His praises. The more fanatical we are, the greater impact we are going to make on this generation. When people see that we are sincere to the core and not playing with religion, they will believe in us.

I believe the great athletic coliseums are not for football and baseball. They are for the last big breath of God! With the great breath of God that is coming, no one is going to get tired. We are going to flow in the dynamics of the supernatural.

You will find from studying the history of Israel and Judah that God blesses by generations. We need a new generation today, and I can see it beginning. We have some of the strongest young men preaching the gospel today that we have ever had.

These young leaders must watch out, however, for the same pitfalls that brought down some of the leaders of past movements: power (pride and ambition), money, and sex. It is so easy to get into pride when God blesses your ministry and to take too much of the credit.

It is so easy to get your mind on material gain. Ministers must be givers, not mostly receivers. In accumulation, there comes an awful thing called greed. In the "lust of the eyes" for possessions, you can lose your relationship for God.

It is so easy to be enticed into an illicit relationship. Most of those whom I know who have fallen into adultery tell me they never intended to do it. The pastor has become such an idol that having sex with him would be the greatest achievement in the lives of a minimum of ten women out of a church of five hundred people.

Most preachers cannot imagine how many women get bowled over by just shaking the preacher's hand. "I shook his hand! He shook my hand! I felt the blood flowing through his hand into mine."

That is the wrong attitude. Preachers are servants of God and servants of the people. They are not great. Only God is great. Joseph in the Bible is a great example for a preacher to follow.

I have tried to use him as an example in my counseling with women. I have no couches in my office. I have four very straight chairs. If a woman wants counseling and cannot bring her husband, I always have had my wife or my secretary sit in while she tells her story.

However, the lessons I have learned from the first spiritual pioneers — those in the Bible — would make more than another book. In this one, I have tried to show what the pioneers of the Pentecostal movement have meant to me. I have tried to show some of the lessons I have learned from them: integrity, organization, humility, and how to handle the power of God, among other things.

When I die, an era will be over, because it seems I am like a bridge overlapping all of the moves of this century. However, I hope to be alive when not just an era, but all of time will be over. I am convinced that I will at least see this last great revival. I would hope that everyone who reads this will pray with me for the manifestation in its fullness of the "latter rain."

It is an honor to be called to the ministry considering the wildness of the human nature as typified by an unbroken donkey. We should be grateful not prideful.

No one comes to the ministry complete in his flesh there will be insecurities, human flaws God knows this but he that could ride an unbroken donkey can change any life.

The disciples of Jesus had their own weaknesses, Peter the most out spoken by far of the disciples tried to convince Jesus not to go to the cross for which he was rebuked, he insisted that he would not deny the Lord after the Lord had told him he was going to be sifted by the enemy, he failed woefully, Peter tried to defend the Lord with a dagger but was fortunate the Lord quickly healed the man whose ear he chopped off, he often talked out of turn. Jesus knew him but still chose him, when Jesus rose from the dead knowing the emotional devastation Peter had experienced sent a special message to him that he had risen and was still his friend.

The other disciples were no better they all had human weaknesses but as we allow him to train and correct us we won't be casualties in the battles of life.

INTIMACY
A donkey must have a close relationship with the rider because the rider may use the simplest of touches to get the attention of the donkey. The rider may speak to the donkey with sounds that make no sense to others but has become a code for them.

One reason there is so much error is that many have not learnt to hear the voice of God, Jesus said my sheep hear my voice. The voice of Jesus will not be opposed to the character of Jesus.

Supposing a child hears his mother's voice and instead of the gentle woman she is, her words are harsh, cruel and demeaning, she would question the authenticity of the voice. When enough time is not spent in the word, in fellowship and worship the clarity of God's voice may be in doubt.

"For as many as are led by the Spirit of God, they are the sons of God. For ye have not received the spirit of bondage again to fear; but ye have received the Spirit of adoption, whereby we cry Abba, Father. The Spirit itself beareth witness with our spirit, that we are the children of God: **Romans 8:14-16.**

The inward witness is a knowing on the inside of the believer that God has placed in us to keep us safe. Some call it a hunch, intuition, premonition but when you are saved God has put this in you to help you and it is a safe guide.

When a believer finds himself in a place where there is error God has placed a mechanism in him to tell he is in the wrong place, the inward witness will cause his peace of God to disappear there will be a restlessness on their inside something won't feel right even if the spectacular things were happening.

It is like a stop sign, a feeling of evil foreboding, and if you are quiet enough the inward witness may even be picked up by you as a voice of your own spirit saying, 'get out, something is wrong'.

A woman in our church had gone outside to escort her friend and her peace became disturbed, she was restless and there was a quiet alarm in her heart which seemed to say to her 'go home now', she returned home and found out she had left her cooking gas on and was in danger of a fire outbreak.

If you are in the right place the inward witness will also confirm to you through the peace within, the rest, joy a release, a green light that suggests to you that you can go on.

During the tsunami, many animals escaped because they were able to use their God given senses to perceive what man could not perceive, they got out of the way of the storm before danger hit, if animals can escape danger, you can do the same. It is distressing that spirit filled people will walk into a cult church and remark that the spirit of God is here. Most times we ignore the witness of the spirit.

This weekend in the U.S I was ministering at a church where I had never been before, I had never seen the pastor, when he and his wife came up for prayer the Lord began to show me they were ministers and had struggled on their own to stay afloat but God was going to give them new strength to carry on the ministry as they returned to serve him. He broke down and wept like a baby.

I later found out he had taken a sabbatical from his church for a year and was just in the process of returning. In another place God supernaturally reconciled a husband and a wife who were living apart, they were both in the service but I did not know who they were, the Lord showed me things about the man's willingness to make things work and were reconciled, tears flowed freely as the estranged wife had been asking the Lord if she were to take the husband back. The voice of God will promote the character and nature of God which is RIGTHEOUSNESS PEACE AND JOY IN THE HOLY GHOST. If you find yourself in a meeting where this godly characteristics are missing and you peace and quiet on the inside is disturbed, pause, listen pray and leave.

"And Peter answered and said to Jesus, Master, it is good for us to be here: and let us make three tabernacles; one for thee, and one for Moses, and one for Elias. Fore wist not what to say; for they were sore afraid. And there was a cloud that overshadowed them, and a voice came out of the cloud, saying, this is my beloved son; hear him. And suddenly, when they had looked round about, they say no anymore, save Jesus only with themselves. And as they came down from the mountain, he charged them that they should tell no man what things they had seen, till the son of man were risen from the dead". **MARK 9:5-9**

But we all, with open face beholding as in a glass the glory of the Lord, are changed into the same image from glory, even as by the Spirit of the Lord. **2 CORINTHIANS 3:18**

The disciples who had been with Jesus on the mountain were changed; they wanted to remain with him on the mountain, although they had walked with him prior to this intimate moment created a hunger for his presence like never before. This time when they were alone with Jesus he was transfigured in their sight.

You can be in the service of God, but each time you're alone with Jesus you can see a different side of his glory. The glory that he brings every time will be different if you learn to be alone with him. Many times, we spend too much time with the people instead of being with Jesus and when you are with Jesus and you see his glory, then you have his presence to bring back to the people.

If your transformation has stopped you have stopped looking at his face. The meat you bring to people can become stale if you're not in the presence of the person who gives the meat. The message we get for the people is received as the face of Jesus shines upon our face then.

Moses went on top of the mountain and the glory of God shone on his face. When he came down the people saw the glory on his face. We are supposed to reflect the glory of God, carriers of that anointing. There's no substitute for being in the presence of God. When you get to a place of spiritual complacency, you stop seeking the Lord, the message dries up and the church becomes an excitement ground, there may be plenty of smoke but no fire.

The church should not be a funeral parlor, because the spirit of the Lord brings freedom, we must not also become an entertainment club where the presence of God is not experienced and excitement takes the place of the move of the spirit.

An unbeliever who walks into a church needs to meet with the presence of God in the church. We should not be so seeker sensitive that we are not Holy-Ghost sensitive, without the presence of God the place is dry; Jesus said no one can come except the father draws them. The ambience created by excellent equipment is not the presence of God. The presence of God is presence of the Holy Spirit that creates reverence and brings freedom to the people. Mental efforts may bring a change of mind, but only the Holy Spirit brings a change of heart, the souls who are converted through this means may reconvert to something else.

HUMILITY

The donkey Jesus rode had unique experiences, people threw their clothes on her back, they threw branches in front of him, they surrounded him, he travelled to Jerusalem, and these were all new to him.

As ministries grow things are added, people pay more attention to the minister, more material things are added, new opportunities come, the minister of God gets to go to places he never dreamt were possible in his life time. In the case of the donkey he was excited but he never took credit. He could not. When God begins to lift we must know that these things are not earned no matter how hard we have worked or what credentials we have, they have only come because Jesus is riding on our back.

Nobody was really worshipping the donkey, they did not care about the donkey, her blessing and fame came because Jesus was there. He is not the celebrity Jesus is. We should all see ourselves as donkeys for Jesus. God calls and beautifies you for his own glory and God adds value to our lives for which we must remain grateful not prideful.

The servant experiences the glory of the miraculous but must immediately give the credit to the Lord.

When this perspective is really understood, you don't need a lengthy introduction and endless titles to have a sense of worth, the donkey only introduced Jesus the donkey is not the focus but the rider.

Several years ago, Dr. Graham was interviewed on PrimeTime Live. The final question was: *"What do you want people to say about you when you're gone?"* His response took many by surprise. *"I don't want people to say anything about me. I want them to talk about my Savior. The only thing I want to hear is Jesus saying, 'Well done, my good and faithful servant.'"* Then he bowed his head and said softly, "But I'm not sure I'm going to hear that."

Dr Billy Graham's answer shows a depth of humility not common, this is a man who has probably preached to more people than any one in his generation, but he recognizes that Jesus is the rider on the donkey and never tried to build a name or an empire. He was kingdom minded not building a personal empire.

"And Saul answered and said Am not I a Benjamite, of the smallest of the tribes of Israel? and my family the least of all the families of the tribe of Benjamin? wherefore then speakest thou so to me"? **1 Samuel 9:21**

When God called Saul, he gave a very humble account of himself and when God called David he said the same thing. At Saul's consecration, he hid among the baggage, but Saul got to a point in his life that he became so successful, and that success got in to his head.

He felt a need to preserve a kingdom he did not earn. Ministry gifts are given by Jesus, Saul wanted to keep himself, maintain popularity and fame, keep the attention of the crowd.

The donkey Jesus rode into Jerusalem had only one purpose to carry the master. She was not moved by the cheers of the people. She enjoyed the moment but stayed focused because without the assignment and the rider there would be no donkey.

"I wrote unto the church: but Diotrephes, who loveth to have the preeminence among them, receiveth us not". **3 JOHN. 9**

There can be the same spirit of pride in the pew not just among the laity or the ministers, people try to function where there is no grace and it leads to disgrace. It is the same kind of spirit we see in Diotrophes, He was a man that wanted eminence rather than to be useful, he even tried to usurp the authority of the Apostle John.

Sometimes people extremely successful in the world want to be stars in the church and they have no calling for those assignments but want to call the shots. Some people put themselves in the lead but if God has not set them up he will put them down.

Ministry is not a career ladder that you climb it is a service that you render. God has not called everyone to lead a church, if the call is not there it would be a struggle, 'owning' a personal ministry as some suppose has become a commercial approach to the kingdom of God.

Satan preferred to be number one in hell than serve God. What is driving the need to be a founder of a ministry is it finances is it fame or is it God? I have had founders of ministry come to ask me if they are called of God. I am always puzzled because if you don't know if you are called of God you really have no business leading anybody.

"And it came to pass after this, that Absalom prepared him chariots and horses, and fifty men to run before him. And Absalom rose up early, and stood beside the way of the gate: and it was so, that when any man that had a controversy came to the King for judgment, then Absalom called to him and said, of what city art thou? And he said, thy servant is of one of the tribes of Israel.

And Absalom said unto him, see, thy matters are good and right; but there is no man deputed of the king to hear thee. Absalom said moreover, oh that I were made judge in the land, that every man which hath any suit or cause might come unto me, and I would do him justice.

And it was so, that when any man came nigh to him to do him obeisance, he put forth his hand, and took him, and kissed him. And on this manner did Absalom to all Israel that came to the King for judgement: So Absalom stole the hearts of the men of Israel". **2 SAMUEL 15:1-6**

The Bible describes Absalom as a handsome, ambitious, arrogant young man who tried to steal the heart of the people from his father. He contested the throne with his father and lost. It is interesting that he was hanging by his beautiful bundle of hair at the end of his life.

The things we refuse to deal with end up destroying us. Absolom and Adonijah tried to take the throne and the consequences were grave. This is one reason why a self-promotion is doomed when there is no backing from God. You may get all the endorsements of the men that be, but if God be against you it doesn't matter who is for you.

Title chasing is sometimes an indication that the minister is insecure or not called at all, there are many self-styled Apostles who have no planted one church, prophets who have not had one clear vision, evangelist who don't know how to win a soul and have healing records, pastors who don't know where the flock is and teachers whose message no one understands but they advertise the title, like someone said seating in your garage and calling yourself a car does not a make you one.

If the call is there and the fruit follows, you don't need all the advertisement and promotions to be known. Titles are changed from year to year as though this is a promotion exercise; usurping spiritual office in the old covenant was sometimes met with instant death.

PURPOSE

The donkey Jesus rode into Jerusalem ended her ministry as soon as Jesus was done with riding her. All of us are in the same situation our ministry are called to fulfill purpose and as soon as we do that the master decides the place, time, duration and extent of ministry.

Moses was a great leader but God showed him the promise land and did not allow him to enter. Abraham sojourned in the land of promise but did not posses it in his lifetime.

I am many times amazed when a great general passes on in the body of Christ and the world does not even take note, the church sometime has a paragraph on their entire life and ministry but we know heaven celebrates her own. It goes to show the transient nature of so called success.

Many great servants of God have passed this way and handed us the batons to run our own course.

I had an experience in 1989, when I was so discouraged, suddenly I was caught up to heaven and there was this great stadium where many saints who had passed over were watching me. All of them knew my name and were calling me in unison encouraging me not to give up. The Bible says we are surrounded by this great cloud of witnesses.

In Hebrew 12:1 the Bible says: *"Wherefore seeing we also are compassed about with so great a cloud of witnesses, let us lay aside every weight, and the sin which doth so easily beset us, and let us run with patience the race that is set before us"*

The Apostle Paul wrote that without us all this great saint will not be complete. This goes to show that God has selected the course everyone is supposed to run. You are born at the right time, in the right season.

Jesus is waiting for the precious fruit of the earth and we must let our heart flow with the heartbeat of God at this time.

And it shall come to pass afterward, that I will pour out my spirit upon all flesh; and your sons and your daughters shall prophesy, your old men shall dream dreams, your young men shall see visions; And also upon the servants and upon the handmaids in these days will I pour out my spirit. And I will shew wonders in the heavens and in the earth, blood, and fire, and pillars of smoke. The sun shall be turned into darkness, and the moon into blood, before the great and the terrible day of the Lord come. And it shall come to pass, that whosoever shall call on the name of the Lord shall be delivered: for in mount Zion and in Jerusalem shall be deliverance, as the Lord hath said, and in the remnant who the Lord shall call. **JOEL 1 2:28-32**

"Be patient therefore, brethren, unto- the coming Of the Lord. Behold, the husbandman waiteth for the precious fruit of the earth, and

hath long patience for it, until he receive the early and latter rain. Be ye also patient; establish your hearts, for the coming of die Lord draweth night. Grudge not one against another, brethren lest ye be condemned: behold, the judge standeth before the door".
James 5:7-8

.

God's purpose at this time is getting the church ready and bringing the harvest in as the return of the Lord Jesus draws closer. .If the last days started on the day of Pentecost (Acts 2:17), we have a right to expect a greater, deeper move of the spirit in this hour. The Bible also teaches that we can hasten his coming (2 Pet 3:12). Jesus also said the gospel will be preached as a sign to every nation.

We saw the breaking down of the former Soviet Union, opening up of Eastern Europe and some of the world's greatest churches are there. A missionary working with pastors in China and countries in Asia reported about meetings where they have half a million pastors in training.

God the father has ordained this so that these countries closed to the gospel will open up there are some other nations that will not break up because it is in staying together that the light of the gospel can reach such nations.

Some will break up to allow the gospel in. We are seeing increased number being saved, good churches being planted and prospering, God is releasing more healings, and miracles and deeper move of the spirit of God on the earth. The gospel in these last days will cost something to be proclaimed, the persecuted church is paying a great price to have the word go forward but resistance is part of the package, we must expect such and brace for it when it occurs, Satan will not yield territories without a fight.

"But none of these things move me neither count I my life dear unto myself, so that I might finish my course with joy, and the ministry, which I have received of the Lord Jesus, to testify the gospel of the grace of God". **Acts 20:24**

Paul was focused on the purpose of God that he was not deterred by distractions, he had an assignment and his assignment had him. Persecution and trouble are part of effective ministry. It seems that Paul' life was from ministry to prison and prison to ministry.

One of our missionaries working in a difficult area, a woman minister who is making extra ordinary impact, she gets arrested and rearrested, she said to me that when she is arrested she sees her time in prison as a time of rest. This kind of thinking is so foreign to many, in fact she rejoiced when she was persecuted. The thinking that the will of God will always be easy will rob us of forward momentum. Paul wrote to Timothy 2 timothy 2:3, he asked him to endure hardness, affliction, trouble as a good soldier.

The concept that there will be no resistance in the ministry is foreign to the New Testament. In fact, persecution had the effect of promoting the gospel.

People who are not ready to endure affliction, trouble will jump ship when persecution hits. In an encounter, I had with the Lord in 1991, he showed me that just before the rapture of the church there were many who mocked the gospel, persecution was rife.

"Thou therefore endure hardness as a good soldier of Jesus Christ. No man that warreth entangleth himself with the affairs of this life; that he may please him who hath chosen him to be a soldier". **2 Timothy 2:3**

I was returning from Eastern Europe recently and someone asked me what I was looking for in such a hard place, this probably explains the situation today with ministry urban migration, where people are seeking their wealthy place rather than the place purpose. There is a big movement of ministers away from rural areas, poor countries to urban and bigger centers, for some it is a quest for easier lives. A person who operates in the covenant of blessing can live and prosper anywhere God has called him.

"And I heard a loud voice saying in heaven, Now is come salvation, and strength, and the kingdom of our God, and the power of his Christ: for the accuser of our brethren is cast down which accused them before our God day and night. And they overcame him by the blood

of the Lamb, and by the word of their testimony; and they loved not their lives unto the death". **Revelation 12:10-11**

This passage speaks about overcoming when we are prepared to lay down our lives, I know many believers who have paid the supreme price, some others face different persecutions daily but the kingdom we have received cannot be shaken.

Satan will send his fiercest attacks from within and without as we approach the end, there will be those who will trouble the church with false doctrines and those who would challenge the freedom of our faith but there will be such an outpouring of the Spirit of God unprecedented.

The early church was filled with glory but the persecution was brutal, the church was born in glory and power and will be raptured in glory and power with persecution.

The early church when faced with persecution were not deterred, we must not develop the attitude that when God is moving, there won't be resistance. The revelation the Lord showed me in 1991, agrees with scripture that in the last days there will be scoffers, what surprised me however was that there were scoffers from within the church.

" This second epistle, beloved, I now write unto you; in both which I stir up your pure minds by way of remembrance: That ye may be mindful of the words which were spoken before by the holy prophets, and of the commandment of us the apostles of the Lord and Saviour: ¶ *Knowing this first, that there shall come in the last days scoffers, walking after their own lusts, And saying Where is the promise of his coming? for since the fathers fell asleep all things continue as they were from the beginning of the creation.* **2 Peter 3:1-4**

Maranatha Come Quickly Lord Jesus

======================